What I Learned From Frogs In Texas

Saving Your Skin With Forward-Thinking Innovation

By

Jim Carroll

Oblio Press, www.obliopress.com

Carroll, Jim, 1959-
 What I learned from frogs in Texas : saving your skin with forward-thinking innovation / Jim Carroll.

ISBN 0-9736554-0-2

 1. Organizational change. I. Title. II. Title: Saving your skin with forward-thinking innovation.

HD58.8.C37 2004   658.4'062
C2004-906489-4

Production Credits:
Editors: Christa Carroll, Janice Dyer
Cover Design and Photography: Franke James
Cover Design and Photography Copyright © 2004 Franke James
www.frankejames.com

Printed in Canada

CONTENTS

C h a p t e r 1 1

Smart Frogs Go Forward

ACKNOWLEDGEMENTS

First and foremost, I should note that this book really had two authors. Given the level of effort that she put in, in terms of content, direction, and subject matter, I tried to convince my wife, Christa, to let me list her as the co-author, but she would have none of it!

Christa took on an unprecedented role in bringing this book to print, through constant analysis of the content, in reworking and reshaping my ideas, and by giving it substance where my efforts were lacking. She spent countless hours in reviewing the ideas I was struggling to get on to paper, crystallized what I was trying to emphasize, and reshaped it back into proper form. Her efforts were remarkable, and I am blessed to have such help.

To Rob Mustard, for his enthusiasm in attacking an early version of the manuscript, and then jumping back in when it was nearing its finish. To Janice Dyer, for her skillful editing. And to Nicola Maher for her passion for detail.

To Franke James and the James Gang, for their brilliant cover design. Innovation is all about taking risks, but I knew when I thought of Franke for the cover that there was little risk involved. Real artist's ship! Learn more about Franke at www.jamesgang.com and www.frankejames.com.

To Reptilia (www.reptilia.org) for donating the time of a variety of frogs for the cover shoot!

To Bill Detlefsen, for providing me with his unique blend of inspiration so many years ago. And Osama Arafat and Mark Jeftovic for sticking with me through the years.

And, last but not least, to those little Texan frogs, for helping me to understand what it is I've been trying to tell people for so many years!

ABOUT THE AUTHOR

Jim Carroll lives five years in the future.

As a leading international futurist, trends and innovation expert, he dedicates his time to helping people and organizations understand how they can aggressively adopt tomorrow, today.

Jim's career began with the world's largest accounting firm some twenty five years ago, an experience that provided him his solid grounding in business strategy. His massively complex curiosity about the world around him led to a rapid career right turn that led to his present day career as a global futurist.

Along the way, Jim has spent a great deal of time writing, speaking, and thinking about trends, change, innovation and opportunity. He has co-authored and authored dozens of books that have sold throughout the U.S., Canada, Germany and India, as well as writing several hundred articles for a wide variety of publications.

Jim and his wife Christa live and work at their home in Mississauga, Ontario, with their two children, Willie and Thomas.

With a combined total of twenty five years of experience of working together in their home office, Jim and Christa are a testament to the fact that a marriage is truly a partnership.

To Christa

*Words cannot define the meaning that you
bring to my life. Without your encouragement,
efforts and insight, this book would not have
existed, nor would I be doing what I am able
to do.*

To Willie and Thomas

*For constantly reminding me that there is
more to life than what I might have ever
known.*

Chapter 1

Squish!

If they don't get off that road, there's gonna'
be a big problem and it's gonna be ugly!

They get squished, you know—the Texan frogs.

It's important to get that issue out of the way, so I can put the most important theme of this book into perspective: it isn't the fact that the frogs get crushed, it's the reasons why.

FROGS IN THE CULVERT

I have been using the story of the frogs in Texas for quite some time to outline why I believe so many seem to be failing when it comes to dealing with the future.

How did the story come about? I was speaking at a conference held at a large, upscale resort in Houston early one autumn. It was a hot, humid, sticky day, typical of the weather at that time of year. As I walked from the conference center to the hotel room (which, being in Texas where "everything is bigger," was quite a hike), I noticed them sitting on the road, in a slight puddle of water. Little green frogs, cute as a button.

In but a moment, they jumped into the culvert at the side of the road. What happened? Some gulls flew in, and conscious of the impending threat, the frogs reacted appropriately.

In a little while, the frogs darted back onto the road. Their goal was to get into the puddle—the hotel sprinkler system was on, and some of the runoff was making its way onto the road. Once there, the frogs spent their time enjoying the water before their natural instinct once again took over: when they spotted a gull in the distance, they jumped right back into the culvert.

> *In Japan, frogs are considered symbols of good luck.*

But they were determined to enjoy their little pond! As soon as they were back in the darkened culvert, you could see their little green eyes looking out, watching carefully. Whenever the gulls left, the frogs jumped out, only to repeat their retreat moments later as yet another avian adversary flew in. This small bit of inconsequential theater occurred throughout the day as I went back and forth from my hotel room to the conference center.

Earlier that morning I had provided the opening keynote for a conference, and had spoken quite forcefully about the fact that many organizations need to start thinking again about the future. I had suggested to the audience that we should take the time to understand the important trends that might affect us through the next five, ten or fifteen years. From that, we can then carefully determine what we might do to respond to some fairly unique challenges, issues and threats set to emerge. It's an important message, and is one that I am often called upon to deliver. The frogs in Texas soon provided me with a unique method of getting that message across.

I had great fun watching these little frogs—until 4 PM when the conference drew to a close.

SHORT-TERM THREATS

I was once again making my way back to my hotel room, and there were my little green friends, sitting in the road, focused on the seagulls. They didn't notice that the conference had come to an end, and that several hundred cars were starting to leave the parking lot. Their demise was dramatically ugly but painfully brief. That's probably a good thing, because they certainly had no idea what was coming. While they were out on the road cavorting around in the puddles and dodging the gulls, they didn't notice the sudden increase in traffic coming from the other direction.

> **Definition**
> *Ranidaphobia: The fear of frogs*

This made me think—the frogs were so busy focusing on the short-term threats and problems, they seemed to give precious little thought to some of the longer-term threats that might present them with even greater challenges.

That's when I clued in to the fact that these frogs in Texas had established a pattern of behavior similar to that of many people in the world today.

FRAME OF MIND

The fact that the frogs were instantly squished into little green bits of nothingness seems tragic, yet what is even more tragic is that they could have seen it coming if only they had taken the time to look beyond "right now." That simple reality seems to match the circumstances of quite a few people in the world today. I see far too many people who are like the frogs on the road in Texas: unaware of the changes occurring around them. They may be extremely focused, but they are looking at the wrong threat, in the wrong direction, at the wrong time.

We need to change our frame of mind with respect to the changes occurring in the world around us, and the trends that will present challenge and opportunity. I believe the pace of change in our world is going to increase, and will be relentless and unforgiving.

I'm convinced that everything we know—the jobs and professions in which we have been trained, the marketplace in which we sell our products, the industries in which we work, and the knowledge we are expected to have mastered—will be extremely different tomorrow compared to where we are today.

> **Science Fiction??**
> *The rate of change is so fast that many science fiction authors argue whether there can be anything such as science fiction.*

Indeed, I'm a big believer that we are now living in a period of time involving the fastest rate of change ever to have occurred, and that rate of change is speeding up. To survive and thrive, we must learn how to anticipate these changes, understand how they might impact us, and learn what we need to do to turn these challenges into opportunities.

I believe this is a critical capability, and it is the focus of this book.

Learning to deal with a world of relentless change can prove to be very difficult and challenging, yet it is also something that can be done. People need to start thinking again about the future. Not a future that comes in the next few weeks or the next few months, or even what might come next year. Instead, people need to start thinking long-term—a type of thinking that seems to have come to an end in the last few years.

Otherwise, they'll find they are not unlike those frogs on the road in Texas.

Chapter 2

What's Wrong?
Aggressive Indecision

"Behold the turtle. He only makes progress
when he sticks his neck out."
James Bryan Conant

Why is it that people have become like the frogs on the road in Texas?

Perhaps because we've been through so much in the last several years. We've had such a perfect storm of negativity that a major shift in attitude has occurred—one that I call "aggressive indecision."

Three recent events have shaped and changed our attitude toward trends and the future. The end result is that we are driven by irrational pessimism, fear of uncertainty and an excessive focus on righting the wrongs of the ethics scandals. We've allowed ourselves and our organizations to drift into a corporate culture and personal attitude in which "doing nothing" is an adequate response to change. Worse yet, we've reduced our willingness to accept risk to such a degree that we seem unable to innovate to keep up with the future.

In other words, the future is rushing at us at a furious pace, and many people are ill-positioned to cope with what it might bring.

ARE YOU SPINNING YOUR WHEELS?

Step back and think about whether you are caught up in the "aggressive indecision" trend. Have you found yourself in any of these situations lately?

- You've been providing clients with a project quote every quarter; when you decide to finally press them to close the deal, they are shocked to learn you've been giving them a regular quote for 2½ years.

- You have a new initiative based on a key business trend that is still on the list of "things to deal with," long after the trend has gone supernova and disappeared. You simply couldn't get the initiative going due to your own inertia or your organization's basic inability to move forward with anything new.

- You finally decided to upgrade some of your significant business systems or manufacturing equipment, only to learn that you've waited so long the system you planned on putting in place is already out of date.

- Your organization identified some significant market threats and challenges, studied them and analyzed them, only to be caught flat-out by failing to respond to those challenges in time because of a lack of an action plan and an inability to make decisions.

Sound familiar? It should. These are but a few signposts of what seems to be the new reality of business today. The "aggressive indecision" attitude has permeated the culture and mindset of many organizations and the individuals who work within them.

This attitude is a relatively recent malaise. There is no doubt that in the last several years, many organizations and individuals have lost their sense of direction. Certainly in the nineties, people had a sense of purpose, a desire to get things done. There was a degree of excitement in the business community, with a belief that anything was possible. *"Nobody knows where we're going, but we're making great time"* could have been the catch phrase.

Now no one knows where they're going, they are taking their time getting there, and many don't even seem to be ready to decide where they want to go!

Lost Momentum

From my perspective, too many people and organizations have lost their momentum; they're stuck in a rut, spinning their wheels. They are ill-equipped to cope with change, and don't have the mindset to fuel future innovation.

> *Symptoms of Aggressive Indecision*
>
> *Few of your business problems have gone away while people have dithered.*
>
> *There is an ingrained corporate culture that supports indecision.*
>
> *People begin to lose the instinct to "trust their gut feelings" and tend to over analyze.*
>
> *Decision makers become more and more dissatisfied with the uncertainty culture, and eventually leave because of frustration.*

It wasn't always this way. Over the last twenty years or so, many organizations invested heavily in creativity and innovation. They recognized that they needed to think and act differently to continue to survive and thrive. They worked hard to adjust for the impact of globalization—increased competition, efficiencies brought about by technology, customer and market upheaval—and a wide variety of other challenges and opportunities. Through rather intense effort, they managed to make their people and the overall organization far more innovative, thus ensuring they could change at the pace the future demanded of them.

Yet, we are now witnessing the annihilation of all those efforts as the culture of aggressive indecision comes to the forefront and dominates the business agenda. What brought about this dramatic change?

IRRATIONAL EXUBERANCE TO IRRATIONAL PESSIMISM

In 1996, concerned about what seemed to be a rather lofty stock market value, Alan Greenspan coined the phrase "irrational exuberance." He was describing the pervasive mindset throughout the business community, and was attempting to caution people that they were perhaps getting too carried away with their expectations regarding the future.

Since that time, we've seen the confluence of three unique events that have forever shaped our willingness to go forward—the perfect storm: the dot-com collapse, 9/11 and ethical scandals. The impact of what has happened is such that we've gone from Greenspan's era of irrational exuberance about the future to one of irrational pessimism.

Consider what each of these three events has done to our ability to deal with the future.

The Dot-com Collapse

The '90s was a remarkable time, as business, government and not-for-profit organizations discovered the power, opportunity and threat from sudden massive global connectivity. The Internet burst into public consciousness in the early '90s as no other technology ever had before, or likely ever will again.

Yet looking back, people got too carried away with the potential for the future; in retrospect, there is no doubt that the hysteria surrounding the 'dot-com' years was rather astounding and ridiculous. As it began to invade our business and personal lives, a period of insanity seemed to take over the world. We witnessed a period of widespread excess, with wild predictions about the future, questionable business models, soaring stock market valuations and lots of media hype.

It was like a party, and we all know what happens when a party comes to an end: a hangover sets in. Clearly, the business world partied hard during the '90s, doing a lot of things in the midst of dot-com hysteria that they would later come to regret. The party came to an abrupt end with the dot-com collapse of March 2000, the subsequent stock market meltdown and the period of gloom that quickly followed. People woke up with a massive, debilitating hangover, which resulted in many of them losing a lot of their innovative spirit.

I quickly saw the signs, as I observed countless people and organizations managing to convince themselves that the future wasn't happening. They concluded that if the dot-com companies were dying a quick death, then certainly a world of massive global connectivity wouldn't have much impact on their business. They became skeptical about any new ideas involving different ways of doing business or supporting and interacting with their customers, or of innovative new ways of restructuring their operations using technology.

They became blind to the fact that we are still in the early stages of a world economy in the midst of an ongoing and massive restructuring—one that involves new ways of working, partnering and cooperating. This 21st Century economy promises continued market upheaval, challenging customer relationships, constant cost reduction and all kinds of new threats and opportunities.

9/11 and Massive Uncertainty

Right after the market downturn of 2000 came 9/11, and the massive psychological impact of a new world in which confidence about the future is forever shaken.

Business decisions have always required a degree of certainty; September 11 changed that in dramatic fashion. The events were so shocking and horrific that they have led us into a future in which fear of the unknown is the guiding principle for many individuals and organizations.

Clearly, 9/11 caused so much uncertainty that many executives are afraid to make decisions because the next unforeseen event might have extremely negative consequences. Uncertainty increases risk, and the mindset brought about by 9/11 has increased the level of risk to an unacceptable degree for many people and organizations.

While we can stop innovating, we can't stop change. The result is that many individuals and organizations need to learn how to reassess and rebalance risk so they can go forward in an era of constant, greater uncertainty.

Governance and Ethics

The third element in our perfect storm? The ethical scandals involving Enron, WorldCom and many other organizations, which only managed to further harm our already shaky willingness to accept risk.

Why is that? Our response to the scandals has been the emergence of a "culture of compliance," an approach that has shifted the focus of many organizations from one of innovation and the future, to one of concentration on the nuts and bolts of today's operational concerns.

> *"Everything you hear, from Sarbanes Oxley to CEOs is 'for God's sake, don't take any risks— don't take a chance.' If that view really prevails, it would put a sure stop to growth and development."*
> *Famed economist Milton Friedman, commenting in an Investors' Business Daily interview*

The biggest impact has been on US-publicly traded companies, who are subject to the many requirements of what is known as the Sarbanes-Oxley legislation. While the act (SOX) currently applies only to American public companies, its effects are far-reaching, touching every type of organization, large and small. Indeed, consultants worldwide are having an extremely busy time in helping out every type of organization to deal with the new culture of compliance that has emerged.

While there are many issues associated with SOX, one of the biggest potential concerns is that it imposes some very strict and very bureaucratic requirements on how organizations operate and manage their operations. No one can argue against the need for improved corporate practices given what went wrong; yet, the effort to comply with the more onerous requirements of SOX is taking away precious management time. Indeed, a tremendous amount of executive talent is now being spent in preparing for and responding to the new paperwork compliance process, instead of concentrating on making money and innovation. How big an effort does compliance involve? *Financial Executive* magazine recently noted that US public companies spent over $1 billion on Sarbanes-Oxley related compliance in 2003. By 2004, they spent even more time and money in dealing with some of the more challenging provisions of the act.

These costs divert limited funds available for innovation and improved efficiencies. Not only that, but the entire process diverts attention away from opportunities for innovation and day to day opportunities, towards paperwork and compliance.

> *Are Companies at War with Themselves?*
>
> *Recent surveys have shown that many major companies have been busy putting in place a Chief Innovation Officer as part of an effort to encourage ongoing innovation. At the same time, one of the fastest growing new corporate positions as a result of Sarbanes Oxley is that of the Chief Risk Officer. One must wonder at the unique culture clash that will occur when the two get together in the same room!*

Yes, compliance and ethics are exceedingly important in today's economy, given the new realities that surround us. Yet it is absolutely vital that you don't permit your organization to suffer as you work to manage the process.

THE DISAPPEARANCE OF OUR RISK BUDGET?

The impact of all of these events has been a dramatic lowering of people's and organizations' tolerance for risk.

A culture of risk is critical to innovation—without it, people will not try to step outside of the box. Without the ability to make mistakes and be rewarded for failure, no one will try anything new. The impact of the dot-com collapse, 9/11 and the intense focus on governance has meant that organizations are seeing a dramatic reduction in their available risk capital.

> *A future oriented leader successfully frames the future in terms of bold contrasts: between the success that comes from innovation and change, and the failure that comes from risk-aversion and unwillingness to change.*

Recently, several bank CEOs raised an alarm about the impact of the new era of ethics, noting that an excess of new rules and regulations could get in the way of a board's ability to focus on risk-taking and creating long-term value. Companies are finding it a struggle to attract and retain talent for their boards, given the compliance issue and the rising cost of directors' liability insurance. Not to mention the fact that the pool of available talent is decreasing as a result of the increased legal risks for directors themselves.

If we destroy the ability for risk and innovation at the board level, it will disappear from the rest of the organization too.

DECISION DEFERRAL AND DECISION AVOIDANCE

The perfect storm has also led to another startling business trend: in an era of uncertainty in which risk culture is disappearing, people have decided to indefinitely postpone making decisions—or are deciding not to make decisions at all! And they like it!

Quite clearly, in an era of skepticism, fear of the future and with the loss of risk capital, both people and organizations have slid into a culture in which it has become completely acceptable to put everything on the "back burner."

Take a look around you—at yourself, your co-workers, your organization, and the business world at large. What do you see?

People mired in the thick mud of aggressive indecision. They tend to wait for absolutely perfect information which will help convince them that the time is right to make a decision, rather than making decisions based on imperfect information as they had done in the past. They'll take a look at the information they have, decide that it's just too darn risky to make a decision on what they see, and do nothing.

The result is an economy in which everyone seems to be stuck in a rut, unwilling and unable to move forward. The fact is, our confidence in the future has been shattered. Corporate nervousness has become the watchword, with the result that everyone is taking the easy way out: deal with uncertainty by doing nothing.

An era of "aggressive indecision": a very dangerous attitude to have, given that organizations must be in a state of continuous innovation in order to cope with the rate of change that now surrounds us.

Chapter 3

What is Innovation?

"The definition of insanity is doing the same thing over and over again and expecting a different result each time."
Albert Einstein

Through the years, I've witnessed many organizations struggle to cope with the constant change that swirls around them. That is why the era of aggressive indecision worries me so—it has caused many organizations to simply not bother to struggle—they've chosen to deal with change by not dealing with it all.

Having watched them carefully, I've come to conclude that too many continue to do little to advance their operations, their revenue and their overall structure through truly innovative thinking.

What I've realized is that there is a simple reason for this: far too many organizations and the people within them really have no idea as to the nature of innovation, and why it is critical in today's day and age.

ARE ORGANIZATIONS REALLY FAILING AT INNOVATION?

In a word, yes! Simply take a look around.

Despite years of cost cutting, many organizations continue to operate with an alarmingly high cost base, with scads of inefficient business processes built into the bureaucracy. A culture encouraging a relentless drive for ongoing efficiency does not exist, and few staff members think about innovative methods to transform the day-to-day operations. Instead, the organization focuses on the slash-and-burn mentality when faced with cost pressures, rather than imagining how to truly transform itself.

> *Are Companies Good at Collaboration?*
>
> *Not really—which indicates a lack of innovative thinking as to how they work. In one survey by Collaborative Strategies LLC, 32% of the time spent by staff during a typical workweek is spent helping others resolve questions. 54% of those questions had not been answered before, and the answers are not captured to any type of accessible knowledge base. Yet 81% of those in the survey believed it was important that companies should be able to share such knowledge.*

Most organizations do little to provide for a real culture of collaboration. As a result, they continue to reinvent the wheel, unable to share ideas and information among their staff. Worse yet, they see valuable information walk out the door every time an employee leaves, losing valuable expertise and leaking insight on a regular basis.

Then there are those organizations in which staff are caught flat-footed when an announcement is made about a major outsourcing initiative or some other significant restructuring. They are surprised when their skills become irrelevant to the organization. Nobody made them aware that a transition from a tactical to a strategic role was critical to their future. Worse yet, there are often no effective professional development programs in place to provide them with the guidance they need to evolve their career in a world of constant change.

Companies consistently excel at infuriating their customers through their inability to provide rapid, effective and intelligent customer service and support. Surveys continue to show that many organizations have still not managed to combine their call center support infrastructure with that of their online presence, which results in a muddled and often challenging customer service experience. In other cases, sales staff has not been properly briefed on the new products or services that the company has brought to market, with the result that questions from customers are often met with blank stares.

As well, many organizations miss all kinds of opportunities to grow their revenue, simply because they've failed to witness the obvious signs of rapid market and product change. They lack an effective trends radar to help them spot the signs of market upheaval well before they begin—all too often, they are caught by surprise.

In other words, most organizations—and the people who work within them—tend to be about as innovative as your average rock.

Why is this so? Because they either refuse to be innovative, or they simply don't know how to be innovative. Which begs the question—do most people simply not understand what innovation is?

I certainly believe that to be true. Even worse, I find that many organizations and the people who work within them don't think they're responsible for innovation, a misperception that can have disastrous results.

WHAT IS INNOVATION?

The problem comes from the fact that for many people, the very nature of the word "innovation" implies R & D (or "research and development"). They think innovation is only for research scientists who toil away in a sophisticated laboratory, trying to develop the next big breakthrough. They think innovation is simply about developing new products and services to take to market, and since that isn't their area of responsibility, it is unimportant to them.

Their understanding couldn't be more wrong.

While new product and service development is certainly a big part of what makes companies successful, it is only a small component of what we might consider the "innovation opportunity."

Truly innovative companies and the leaders and staff within them realize that innovation can occur with anything: operations, customer service, business processes, the ability to enter new markets, revenue enhancement opportunities, corporate and workplace structure, corporate culture and attitudes and just about everything else!

Innovation is about everything an organization does—and how it does it.

DO YOU HAVE AN INNOVATION PROBLEM?

Of course, you won't have any innovative thinking if you've got a culture that stops fresh thinking in its tracks.

Pause, for a moment, and think about how you or your organization responds to new ideas. Does anyone ever respond with the reaction "we can't do that, because we've always done it this way!" If someone dares suggest something different, does someone inevitably react by saying, "that's the dumbest thing I've ever heard!" Are new initiatives met with the comment "it won't work!"

If so, you've got precious little innovation oxygen fuelling your fire for the future. You need to work hard to fix that problem! A good way to start is by developing an understanding of exactly what is meant by the word "innovation."

THREE SIMPLE IDEAS

The essence of innovation is really quite simple. It is all about coming up with new ideas that help you to run the business better, grow the business and transform the business. But it isn't just about idea generation—innovative companies excel at implementing these ideas and making them work.

Let's examine each of these areas.

Run the Business Better

There is plenty of opportunity in every organization for operational innovation; that is, doing what you can to "run the business better." This type of innovation involves a continuous effort to change, improve and redefine business processes, whether they involve customer service, HR practices, logistics and shipping methodologies, purchasing processes or just about anything else.

Never think there isn't huge room for improvement—most organizations are inherently inefficient, with outdated or illogical processes in place. There is countless potential for improving the way organizations work, and plenty of opportunities for innovative thinking with respect to the way things are done.

Add it up and look at the benefits from doing things smarter or more effectively and there can be a huge return.

Grow the Business

Second, make sure you understand the opportunities from "growing the business," or what might also be called "revenue-focused innovation."

Most often, new revenue comes from new products and the ability to enter a new marketplace. Yet that isn't the only way to enhance revenue. Think about business model innovation, for example: new business ideas involving expansion in existing markets or new ways of reaching the customer that weren't previously possible (or that no one had thought of before).

Revenue enhancement can also come from changing the nature of existing products, such as adding a service component to a product that can bring in additional revenue. It might involve enhancing the perceived image of a product so it is more valuable to the customer, resulting in the customer being willing to pay more for it.

The key is, don't think about "growing the business" and revenue enhancement as simply coming from new products or new markets; there are plenty of other methods for innovative thinking that can lead to revenue enhancement.

Transform the Business

Last but not least, always keep in mind the concept of "transformational innovation."

Transformational innovation involves taking a look at the way the organization is structured, and thinking how it might be able to work smarter, more efficiently and with better results by changing the skills makeup of the organization. It involves constant, probing questions that continually assess the organization and its skills, such as:

- Do we have the people we need in the right places/positions?

- Do we have the right people with the right skills available at the right time?

- If we are suddenly faced with rapid market change, do we know how to access specialized skills and talent we might need?

With the global connectivity that has emerged over the last few decades, there is plenty of opportunity to do today what couldn't have been done even five years ago, in terms of how an organization accesses the skills, resources, talents and capabilities that it needs to get the job done.

Organizational transformation also recognizes the concept of "partnership" as a key corporate structure for the future. In a world of mammoth complexity and constant change, organizations must focus on their core competencies and partner with others to accomplish the things they cannot or should not do. In essence, they must recognize that the path to the future is to concentrate on what they do well and on what is critical to their central mission, and to seek partners to help out with everything else.

TRUCKERS ARE INNOVATORS!

It is entirely possible to pursue an innovation strategy encompassing all three areas of opportunity. If you begin thinking about innovation from these three perspectives, you'll come to realize there are extensive opportunities coming from innovation.

Some of the most innovative organizations that have accomplished all three objectives happen to work within the trucking industry.

Truckers? Did an image just spring to mind?

If so, drop that image, because the trucking industry has been at the forefront of what we might call the "logistics innovation revolution": an effort involving operational efficiencies, revenue growth and organizational transformation, all in one swoop.

Over the last ten years, a wide variety of trucking and shipping companies—ranging in size from mammoth organizations such as FedEx and UPS to the smallest of local carriers—have been at the forefront of an effort to reduce their cost base, grow their revenue and transform their line of business. They've been doing this with the overall strategic objective of assisting their customers in the transformation of their own business operations.

Collectively, they grabbed on to a simple premise: trucking companies could increase the value of their product and service if they helped their customers run their business better. They could transform their own operations and those of their customers by taking on the role of business partner to their clientele. One of the ways they have done this is by layering a service element on top of their basic business model.

Look at what trucking companies offer today: simple tools that allow their customers to build efficiency into the process of arranging for and tracking shipments. These tools allow the trucking companies to reduce their own cost of doing business, which is the idea of "running the business better," or operational transformation.

Sophisticated planning software helps them maximize the load on their departing trucks. In addition, many companies have developed systems to help them schedule last minute or partial loads for immediately departing trucks, which they offer to clients at a reduced rate. Both of these strategies, along with other innovations, have helped them to grow their revenue.

> ### What Defines a Successful Innovation Culture?
> * *Risk taking*
> * *Rule breaking*
> * *Mistakes don't bear dire consequences*
> * *Leaders aren't isolated from ideas*
> * *There's a willingness to learn from failure*
> * *There's no denial as to how much change is happening*
> * *There is a sense of urgency as to the need for change*

They also determined there was an opportunity to transform the very nature of what they do: they could take over the entire shipping operations of many of their client organizations, which led them into the "logistics" business. They've transformed themselves into an effective partner with their clients, and have achieved transformational innovation.

Trucking companies today tend to be some of the more innovative companies on the planet. Not surprising, given that their strategies place them square in the middle of each of the three main innovation opportunity areas.

We can learn from their attitude and their approach, because the frame of mind they have adopted is critical, given what comes next in terms of the trends that will impact us.

C h a p t e r 4

Certain Things are Certain- Eight Big Trends to Think About

*"The rapid industrialization of the
Chinese economy has occurred in only decades,
whereas in Europe the same transformation
took hundreds of years."*

Dr. Alan Thomas,
Australian Ambassador to China

I spend a huge amount of my time looking at the world around me to understand the major trends that will shape our world. In doing so, I attempt to separate the real, significant trends from passing fads. There is no shortage of trends that might impact us; yet I believe there are eight big trends that will have the largest impact on everything we do in the coming years.

> ### The Eight Big Trends
> - *The impact of ever-growing sapiential circles*
> - *An increase in what you need to know*
> - *Rapid scientific advance*
> - *China and the commoditization of human capital*
> - *Change de-resistance*
> - *Changing relationships*
> - *A smarter type of thing*
> - *The skills shortage and end of retirement*

THE IMPACT OF EVER-GROWING SAPIENTIAL CIRCLES

Perhaps the most significant current trend involves the ever-widening "sapiential circles" that are a part of our daily personal and professional lives.

The phrase "sapiential circles" comes from observations by anthropologist Margaret Mead about how groups generate knowledge within their community; the larger the group, the more knowledge is exchanged. A well-known professor of business at the University of Southern California, Dr. Warren Bennis, later adapted the phrase when he wrote a groundbreaking article entitled *The Secrets of Great Groups*, in which he defined the attributes of successful teams and how they come together to do "great things." He referred to the power of information exchange within a group as being one of its core reasons for success.

In my own case, I've come to use the phrase to describe a group of people who share a common interest in a topic. A "sapiential circle" might consist of a group of doctors interested in recent advances in the treatment of a particular disease; a group of engineers involved in researching leading-edge design concepts; or even marketing specialists interested in sharing information on the latest trends in brand management. All of these groups might be considered sapiential circles, in that they thrive on sharing information on a topic that is near and dear to their heart.

Prior to 1990, most sapiential circles were small, cumbersome and rather slow to share information and generate knowledge. The medical community distributed information in print-based peer-reviewed journals, which provided for a rather slow, leisurely dispersion of new medical knowledge throughout the global community. Researchers of robotics and intelligent systems tended to do the same, with their information-sharing enhanced by the regular exchange of ideas and information at annual professional conferences. Individuals involved in the development of new consumer electronic goods tended to share their information through print-based industry publications and through occasional feedback from their customers, distributors and wholesalers. Chemists, too, had their own circles, as did every other profession and area of scientific endeavor.

In many cases, it was impossible for individuals interested in a particular topic to find and participate in a sapiential circle, beyond reading various publications and newsletters, or by attending the occasional conference. The result was a fairly low level of information exchange, which meant that the world, while evolving rapidly, still moved at a relatively slow pace.

Then something magical happened. Fuelled by the connectivity of the Internet, the very essence of the sapiential circle changed forever. We witnessed massive growth in the reach of the many existing sapiential circles, and the formation and birth of countless new circles. Sapiential circles could now expand worldwide, and draw in countless numbers of new members. Suddenly, we had a vehicle that supported and encouraged the direct distribution of knowledge and information among people on a scale never before witnessed in human history.

Our sapiential circles grew, and they continue to grow.

What is the impact? As our sapiential circles have grown, so too has the overall level of knowledge available to the community. Our sapiential circles have been transformed by global connectivity, and so too has the rate by which information on new developments is shared within the community.

These two facts alone, more than anything else, have led us to a world in which the pace of change is speeding up to a remarkable degree.

AN INCREASE IN WHAT
YOU NEED TO KNOW

Ever-widening sapiential circles and rapid information distribution have led us to an era of exponential knowledge growth.

Consider this statistic: it is estimated that all of the knowledge we have today is but 1% of what will exist in 2050. According to a recent study out of the University of California (Berkeley), we now produce as much new information every six months as was produced in the first 300,000 years of human existence. The result is that every industry, profession and job is impacted by all kinds of new developments, new research, and new information.

The impact on every profession, career, marketplace and industry is stunning. For example, it is estimated that medical knowledge is doubling every eight years, with the result that most medical specialists struggle to keep on top of but a fraction of the new developments. In particular, family physicians can barely keep up; much of their non-office time must now go toward studying and learning the vast number of new medical developments and treatments. Are they succeeding? Likely not.

Ever-expanding sapiential circles are having a tremendous impact on other science-based professions as well. One study suggests that half of what students learn in their freshman college year about science and technology is obsolete or revised by their senior year. Another professional estimate suggests that the half-life of an engineer's knowledge is about five years, and as low as two or three years for a computer professional.

It's not just science-oriented careers that are affected. Individuals in marketing and public relations are finding that growing sapiential circles are leading to new methods of bringing attention to their products. Not only that but they are discovering that they provide unique ways to undertake a brand repositioning. The shelf life of a "great idea" in such an industry in the past might have been a year or two; it can now be measured in weeks.

Farmers too are being impacted. While our image of them might involve a lonely individual on a tractor tilling fields, they must now become experts in the latest trends involving soil analysis, seed application technology and how best to marry new leading-edge fertilizers to particular strains of crops.

> ***Present and Future Changes***
>
> - *Every 2 or 3 years the knowledge base doubles.*
> - *Every day 7,000 scientific and technical articles are published.*
> - *Satellites orbiting the globe send enough data to fill 19 million volumes in the Library of Congress – every 2 weeks.*
> - *High school graduates have been exposed to more information than their grandparents were in a lifetime.*
> - *Only 15% of jobs will require a college education, but nearly all jobs will require the equivalent knowledge of a college education.*
> - *There will be as much change in the next three decades as there was in the last three centuries.*
>
> *Leadership and Technology, National School Boards Association's Institute for the Transfer of Technology to Education*

This trend impacts everything: there will be more opportunities for innovation; careers, markets and organizations will be in a constant state of change; and you will need to learn faster and think more strategically than ever before.

RAPID SCIENTIFIC ADVANCE

Rapid knowledge growth, driven by ever widening sapiential circles, is fuelling rapid scientific advance at a pace we have never witnessed before. With new knowledge comes new discoveries and new innovation—and with this, comes ever more rapid change.

You think the world around you changes quickly now? You haven't seen anything yet.

I recently read a mind-boggling article published in the *Journal of Chemical Knowledge*. The article commented on the challenges faced by chemists and chemical engineers in simply keeping up to date with the "world of the new," noting that:

- to be up-to-date in all areas of chemistry, you currently have to read about 2,000 new publications every day;

- if you prefer to screen only the short abstracts, you must read 200 pages per day, or about 70,000 pages per year;

- furthermore, since the number of chemistry publications is increasing exponentially, you need to double your reading capacity within the next 15 years;

- you must read 20 publications every day to grasp only 1% of the overall new knowledge covered in all these chemical publications!

The article went on to note, "...the number of known chemical substances has been growing exponentially since 1800, from some hundreds then to about 19 million today."

> ***Rapid Advancements in Joint Replacement Surgery***
> *An example of the rapid rate of advancement in medical science can be seen with what has occurred with joint replacement surgery:*
> - *1973 joint replacement introduced, average operating time 140 minutes, average hospital stay 12 ½ days*
> - *1993 average operating time 60 minutes, average hospital stay 5 ½ days*
> - *2003 average operating time 45 minutes or less, average hospital stay 4 days or less.*
> *BBI Newsletter, November 2003*

That's a pretty big leap—but it's insignificant compared to what is coming. The discovery of new chemical compounds is growing faster than ever before. Indeed, the rate of discovery of new chemical substances is now doubling every 13 years. That means that by 2025, chemists will be dealing with some 80 million substances, and by 2050, 300 million. Watch the trend further, and it means that in less than 100 years, chemists will be dealing with 5 billion known substances.

How will this impact you? Everything we do is touched by science. If the essence of science is entering a period of hyper-change, then we too are entering that world. This example from the science of chemistry is but one example of the rapid scientific advance occurring all around us. Look into any field of research and you witness similarly stunning rates of discovery.

CHINA AND THE COMMODITIZATION OF HUMAN CAPITAL

If all of this seems to be a challenge, then let's toss China and the rest of Asia into the mix.

> *Made in China*
>
> *Most people already know that China dominates global manufacturing, but you might not know just how big they are in certain industries.*
>
> *A typical story told in China involves an executive who travels to America on business, and returns home with some expensive toys for the kids that they had obviously never seen before.*
>
> *"But Dad, these were made in China!" they cry.*
>
> *Why would they react this way?*
>
> *Because while China is responsible for 70% of all global toy production, over 80% of that is sold to foreign markets.*

A recent column in the *Electronic Engineering Times* noted that Chinese and Indian universities now award more science and technology degrees every year than America. This means a huge influx of new talent into the global science innovation pool, and the entrance of millions more into our world of global sapiential circles. That fact alone is one of the most significant trends that will impact our future.

Yet, it isn't solely in the area of rapid scientific advance that China will have a massive impact. We are witnessing a nation of over one billion people making a dramatic leap from peasantry to middle-class in as short a time span as fifty years. As more and more Chinese people become employed and further their education, a huge and pent-up demand is emerging for everything the modern world offers them.

That alone will account for upheaval, challenge and opportunity for every business organization—you can expect the Chinese consumer market to be one of great interest. But don't strictly think of China as a market: it is also set to become a massive competitor in every industry, every marketplace and every field of endeavor.

Imagine the reaction of a group of farmers I spoke to recently, when they learned that China is already the world's largest grower of wheat. This is but one example where they have become a major competitor in a global market, and it is a trend that is set to play out in every marketplace. This fact should really come as no surprise for a nation of 1.4 billion people—1 out of approximately every 4 humans on the planet.

What the trend really comes down to is the stunning amount of manpower that China brings to the world as it becomes a mainstream part of the global economy. The sheer size of their workforce leads to what I call the "commoditization of human capital." China is set to become the world's low-cost producer, and that fact alone is going to cause ongoing upheaval for every profession, job, career, industry and marketplace.

> **Chinese Production!**
> *Wal-Mart purchased $12 billion worth of Chinese products in 2002, which represented 10% of all U.S. imports from that country. Some experts claim that up to 70% of all Wal-Mart products come from China.*

China offers the world so much inexpensive, readily available labor, that not only is China set to continue its dominance as the "world's outsourcer" in the manufacturing sector, it will also take on a similar role in every other sector. We are set to see much of the processing, office and professional services of many organizations move to China, where they can be undertaken at a fraction of the price. We will witness the decimation of entire professions, as the value of their skills and capabilities are commoditized.

In thinking through this trend, it is critical to realize that it isn't just China that will see regular commoditization of human capital value; other countries will also have a profound impact on the North American economy. Goldman Sachs predicts that by 2025, the economies of Russia, Brazil, India and China will grow such that they will equal 50 percent of the six largest industrialized (G6) countries. That's up from 15 percent today, and indicates a pretty staggering growth rate. Not only that, but by that point, their combined Gross Domestic Product (GDP) will have overtaken the combined GDP of the G6 countries.

> *Observations on China from Dr. Alan Thomas,*
> *Australian Ambassador to China*
> * *China's GDP in 2003 made it the 7th largest economy in the world.*
> * *In terms of purchasing power, it is the 2nd largest economy in the world.*
> * *Its share of world trading is at about 7% which is 3 times what it was 10 years ago.*
> * *Its economy will be the size of Germany by 2010 and will rival Japan by 2030.*

CHANGE DE-RESISTANCE

Sapiential circles, the growth of knowledge, rapid scientific advance and the commoditization of human capital—we are in for a wild ride, and certainly a lot of change.

And yet, history teaches us that many people are simply averse to change. Ogden Nash brilliantly put this into perspective when he observed that for many people, "progress is great, but it has gone on far too long." That phrase, perhaps more than any other, sums up what we have witnessed in the workplace in the last few years as the baby boomer generation has had to cope with new ways of working, new business models, constant career upheaval, the end of the career for life and everything else that has been thrown at them.

The defining characteristic in the business world for the last twenty or thirty years has been change resistance, perhaps because this is the only generation that has witnessed first-hand the gut-wrenching twists and turns from the introduction of technology into the workplace. The business world has spent gazillions of dollars on workshops, seminars and courses to help these folks "deal with change." Change management has been a significant concern, and entire forests have been cut down to publish lengthy books on how to best incorporate change within an organization.

> ### How Far Apart are Boomers and Gen-Y in Their Mindset?
> *Think about it this way: they are 5 technology generations apart when it comes to what they first used to listen to music. Many Boomers first listened to music on LP records: many of today's youngest Gen-Y will first listen to music on an MP3 player, having never even encountered cassettes, 8-tracks and possibly even CDs.*

Yet the era of change-aversion is coming to an end, and we are entering the time of change-embracement, or change de-resistance. There are two reasons for this. First and foremost, baby boomers are getting better at dealing with change. They've been through quite a lot, and have come to accept that their remaining work years will include continued upheaval and turmoil. Years past, they might have fought the change; today, they are increasingly able to accept it, work with it and do what is necessary to turn change into an opportunity.

In addition, change de-resistance will also be driven by the entrance of Gen-Y into the workplace. Born between the years 1977 to 1999, they make up almost one-quarter of the entire population. While there has been a lot of news coverage about Gen-Y, most of it has focused on marketing and consumer issues, with no shortage of statistics on how much they spend, or how they influence their parents' spending.

Yet there hasn't been a lot of thought given to the impact this unique generation will have on the way we work, and upon the acceptance of change.

Gen-Y is certainly technologically adept, and is of a mindset that if you don't have knowledge about something, you simply enter a few keystrokes to go and get it. They've grown up in a world surrounded by regular change in everything they know—heck, the typical 19 year old has grown up with 4 different generations of gaming technology.

Gen-Y has grown up in a world which is far more complex than that of previous generations, and one in which change has been constant and relentless. They've developed a mindset that is creative, curious and quite used to dealing with the complexity of change. This means that with the Gen-Y crowd, we will likely witness a mindset that thrives on innovation, and one that embraces change in all of its various forms.

Add it all up, and we've got a world that is ever more ready to embrace the change being thrown at it.

CHANGING RELATIONSHIPS

It's probably a great thing that people are more welcoming to change, because we are already in the midst of the most significant yet least understood trend, one that involves a change in the very nature of relationships throughout society.

Let's come back to the issue of sapiential circles; as they've expanded, so too has the rate of knowledge, science and innovation. Another aspect of ever-widening sapiential circles has to do with the fact that they cause some fundamental and long-lasting changes in the way people deal and interact with each other. Examined alone, there are many small signs of changing relationships throughout society that probably don't mean too much. But taken together, they suggest broad implications for everything, ranging from consumer markets, to workplace and corporate models, as well as career and family issues, not to mention political and other trends.

What's going on? There are many foundations upon which relationships have been built, and these foundations are now undergoing significant changes as a result of widening sapiential circles. As the world becomes a smaller place, relationships change.

Consider, for example, the centuries-old relationship between doctors and their patients. For as long as there has been a medical profession, people have turned to and relied upon their doctor for all matters of advice pertaining to their health care. The doctor was the final and sole arbiter of all things medical, was in possession of all the information, and knew exactly what to do for any particular medical situation.

In this relationship, patients rarely, if ever, questioned doctors or challenged their assumptions and decisions. Then in the 1990s, individuals were provided with the ability to seek information on their own—and suddenly, the relationship between doctor and patient began to change. People armed themselves with all kinds of information prior to going into the doctor's office, and were now prepared to question, analyze and dispute what the doctor might tell them. They could reach out through their own sapiential circles to other patients in similar circumstances, seeking advice and guidance for their own unique circumstance. Given the vast growth of medical knowledge, they could even extend their sapiential circle to specialized medical professionals anywhere on the planet.

The result? Doctors were suddenly confronted with a significant change in the professional relationship they were accustomed to, and many weren't quite sure how to react.

That's but one example of a fundamental change in a relationship in society, and it is occurring everywhere as people empower themselves with the rapid explosion of knowledge and the daily shrinking of the planet. (There is a downside of course; sometimes too much knowledge is a bad thing. Certainly, doctors have encountered this as their patients come across fraudulent, misleading information. Yet, having said that, something fundamental has changed in the relationship.)

Let's take the idea one step further. Beyond the change occurring with the ever-widening sapiential circles, there are signs indicating many other changing relationships throughout society. Consider, for example, the relationship between parents and their children.

It used to be that children went away to university, graduated and never came back, except to visit. That is now no longer the case, as a new "boomerang generation" emerges in society. These are the kids who, after graduation, move back home to live with mom and dad. I first observed this trend in the mid-'90s in my own neighborhood, and began to look for statistics, studies and reports suggesting it was a real trend taking hold.

> *"They're Back!"*
>
> *American Demographics magazine reports that more than half of today's 21 year olds still live at home, the highest percentage ever recorded.*
>
> *MonsterTRAK.com found in a survey that 60% of college kids plan on moving back home after graduation.*

And indeed it is; my trends-tracking system soon made it obvious that this was a trend with "legs." One British survey found that one-quarter of parents now expect to be supporting their children until their children are into their 40s! An Australian study showed a similar type of trend: 52 percent of men and 39 percent of women in their late 20s still live at home, and 22 percent of sole-parent families move back home, compared to 6 percent in 1996. In the US, the Census Bureau reports that over 18 million adults between the ages of 18 and 34 still live with their parents. That's an increase of 44 percent since 1970.

Part of the reason for the emergence of the boomerang generation is economic in nature; graduates today don't have the career and job certainty that graduates had in the past. The result is they need a bit more time to get on their feet and get established, and where better to do that than in the warm cocoon of their parent's home? Interestingly enough, surveys show that the current generation gets along better with their parents than many previous generations, which is probably also helping to fuel this trend.

That's but one example of where relationships are changing in terms of families; dig deeper, and you can find additional evidence signaling a fundamental shift in the very nature of the family. For example, in Australia, according to an article in *The Age*, grandparents provide 80 percent of all child care, and half of all families live within thirty minutes of their parents.

There are even more relationship changes swirling around us. As consumers, we have become more empowered and have changed the way we deal with companies that sell to us. We are armed with more information than ever before as we buy a new car, a new home, a new appliance. In the past, we relied on sales staff to give us comparison information, leading us to believe we were getting "the best deal." But with the resources we have available today, sales staff take on a different role; they are more of a partner in our decision to buy something, rather than being strictly a smooth-talking salesperson. Once again, that's a fundamental relationship change.

Up to this point in time, our society has been defined by a solid foundation for various types of relationships; the nuclear family, the job for life, the concept of customer loyalty and membership in a professional association, to name but a few. Yet what is happening now is that these relationships are more tenuous; they are shifting, reforming and reconstructing themselves into something altogether different.

It is by discovering how relationships are changing and how these new relationships can be exploited that opportunities can be found and threats can be determined.

A SMARTER TYPE OF THING

It should be clear by now that the size of the sapiential circles we have with other humans is changing, and changing relationships are one of the key trends affecting our society.

But what happens as your own sapiential circle expands even further, extending itself to the many "things" that surround you in your day-to-day life?

In the next few years, you are going to see a significant change in the many things that you use on a day to day basis, whether they be in your homes, hospitals, offices, factories and just about everywhere else. Two things are going to happen—they are going to become "smart" as a result of rapid advances with intelligent systems and robotics. And they are going to become "plugged in" in very unique ways, such that you will be able to interact with them in ways that you might never have previously imagined.

Intelligent systems? Robotics? Interaction? Isn't that the Jetsons?

If that's what you're thinking, then you're missing one of the most significant advances yet to come in society. As Rodney Brooks, leading robotics researcher at the Massachusetts Institute of Technology observed, "in just 20 years the boundary between fantasy and reality will be rent asunder…Just five years from now that boundary will be breached in ways that are as unimaginable to most people today as daily use of the World Wide Web was 10 years ago."

> **Smart Packaging**
>
> *Scientists at Kraft's NanoteK consortium (an alliance of 15 universities exploring how nanotechnology can aid food production) can see a time, in the not so distant future, when tiny sensors will be embedded into food packaging that will be able to tell us when the contents are no longer edible.*

Over the next several years, we will witness the embedding of "intelligence" into a whole variety of everyday things. At the same time, these everyday things will become connected to the vast information grid that has become so much a part of our world. The result is that your sapiential circle is now going to extend to a lot of smart, interconnected stuff!

On stage, I always tell a little joke as to where this new world might lead us; I might get on my weigh scale one morning, only to realize that it has just sent an e-mail to my fridge, instructing it to deny me entry for the day because I'm just a pound or two over.

While it is good for a chuckle, the story doesn't really demonstrate the reality of what is emerging as the result of the rapid evolution

> **Going Up?**
>
> *A leader in the integration of remote diagnostics and management into the end product is Schumacher Elevator Co., a family-owned and operated manufacturer based in Iowa. They have been working to integrate remote diagnostics and management connectivity into each of the elevators located at their 2,500 installations. They can easily undertake remote diagnostics of their equipment, as well as apply updates, fixes and undertake routine logic maintenance. One objective of this effort is to lower the overall cost of maintenance, allowing them to be more cost-competitive within their industry.*

of science in this area. Here are just a few examples of the types of things that are being developed.

Consider the robotic highway cone shepherd and its flock—a story indicative of the smart world soon to become a routine part of our day-to-day lives.

If you've ever driven on a congested highway undergoing a lane closure, you might not be surprised to learn that some $100 billion US is lost every year through accidents and delays in such situations. The researchers at the University of Nebraska-Lincoln are hoping to improve this statistic by developing intelligent highway cones that can close a lane faster, with far less safety risk.

How does it work? A "shepherd" cone and its "flock" of seven other cones are automatically lowered onto the road by a specially-designed truck. Using GPS (global positioning system) satellite technology, the "shepherd" cone determines the exact location where it was dropped off, and then moves itself to the exact location it needs to be. It then "instructs" its flock to position themselves along the road at specified intervals. All of this is done using advanced, intelligent technology and its connectivity to satellite and radio systems.

Another area in which we can expect many advances is in the world of health care. Forget biomedicine, and think bio-connectivity!

Intel is working on research that might help someone stricken with Alzheimer's "interact with life." Alzheimer's is a tragic disease that often requires intensive caregiver involvement to help patients deal with everyday challenges. Intel is redesigning everyday devices by building into them smart, connected intelligence that will help to remind patients about how to deal with everyday things. They see a future involving programmable coffee mugs, shoes, plates—all of which become smart devices, reminding patients, for example, when to take a particular medication, or simply reminding them how to use something. These types of devices will be particularly helpful to caregivers as rapid advances in medical science have lengthened the life expectancy of their Alzheimer's patients.

Science fiction? Perhaps, but these types of futuristic systems are being researched and developed now. We can expect the arrival of all kinds of whacky and wonderful ideas like these, well into the future.

The next ten to twenty years are going to see a lot of very sophisticated, intelligent and connected systems becoming a part of our day-to-day lives, a trend that will affect the very nature of a wide variety of industries, not to mention having a big impact on what we do every single day.

> *Routine Robotics*
>
> *In the world of heavy industry and manufacturing, intelligence has already changed the very nature of how work is performed. General Motors, for example, already uses some 25,000 robotic devices throughout its manufacturing facilities, performing many routine and often dangerous tasks.*

We will see a lot of automation of routine procedures, particularly with manufacturing assembly lines and other industrial applications. We will see a significant change in terms of home and building design, as smart systems come to play a greater role in such things as home energy usage. The type of consumer appliances that we use will undergo a significant change as it becomes a part of the interconnected, intelligent grid in our home and offices. Our cars will learn to link to embedded, intelligent road flow management sensors that are built into the highway infrastructure, and will provide us with a variety of potential decisions as to alternate routes that we might take.

Yes, it all sounds like science fiction, but this hyper-connectivity and hyper-intelligence is being built today.

THE SKILLS SHORTAGE AND THE END OF RETIREMENT

Another challenging issue you will face through the next decade will be an increasing inability to access the staff and skills necessary to effectively run your business.

> **Loss of Organizational Memory?**
> *An interesting side-effect of the looming retirement of baby boomers is the loss of "organizational memory." Even as organizations witness a knowledge explosion as described earlier in this chapter, they will also see a lot of important and useful knowledge walk out the door as baby boomers retire. Capturing and transferring this knowledge is an important strategy for the future.*

There are several reasons why this is set to become an issue. Looming large is the emerging wave of retiring baby-boomers, a trend that will take a huge amount of relevant and useful knowledge and skills out of the economy. Adding to the problem will be the challenge of recruiting members of Generation-Y for long-term career positions, given they have very different concepts of careers and work/life balance. And last but not least, rapid knowledge growth and hyper-innovation is leading to a world in which the skills you need will become ever more specialized—and ever scarcer.

Baby Boomers Exit the Economy

The first issue is a significant one; quite simply, a lot of specialized expertise is set to exit our workforce as baby boomers begin to retire. In the area of health care, it is expected we will see a shortage of up to 400,000 nurses in the US by 2010. This will be happening just as the health care system finds itself under increasing strain as those same aging baby boomers begin to place additional demands on the health care system.

> **Are You Going to Retire?**
> *An important trend to keep an eye on is the potential "end of retirement." Retirement used to be a one-time event—something you did at the age of 65. In the future, retirement will increasingly become a gradual process taking many, many years to unfold. The best way to think of the trend is to realize that individuals will go through a transitional period from a life of full-time employment to one of full-time retirement—with a lot of a time mixed in between.*

Another example comes from the US Bureau of Labor Statistics, which estimates that over the next ten years, demand for electricians will outstrip supply by 23 percent (or 154,000 workers). That type of reality is looming in every industry, profession and trade. What this means is that we will soon find ourselves in a situation where we are unable to access and find the talent we need to get the job done.

> **Retirement Signposts?**
> *A Towers Perrin survey of 2000 workers finds:*
> * *78% want to continue working in some form in their retirement years*
> * *64% expect to be working part-time*
> * *43% want to keep working simply so they can stay active*

An interesting twist to this retirement issue is that many baby boomers will have a lot of time to kill, and may find they are having difficulties financing their "golden years." As a result, many may head back to the workplace, doing part-time or freelance-type work.

> *Home Depot has formed a partnership with the American Association of Retired People to recruit and hire workers for 1,700 stores.*

Gen-Y Brings Attitude into the Economy

As if that didn't make things challenging enough, we may find that the potential pool of replacements known as Gen-Y might not want to work for us on a long-term basis.

They are the first generation to grow up in a massively interconnected world—they've been weaned on Internet chat services such as ICQ and MSN, have mastered Nintendo and Xbox from an early age, and have never known a world with less than a few hundred TV channels.

This brings a unique challenge that the corporate sector hasn't really had to deal with before: an entire generation of workers who can become extremely bored, extremely quickly! Because they are used to a world in which they can do multiple things at once, and in which their minds are always very active, they'll come to expect the same degree of heightened stimulation in the workplace. They'll have to be provided with a regular stream of new projects and varied assignments and responsibilities. Not only that, they will have to be provided with a career path that allows for multiple different jobs and careers throughout their lifetime.

Even that might not mean they will stay for very long. Consider this statistic which I came upon while doing research for a recent presentation: when asked about a long-term job, newly-graduated consulting engineers thought of a 2 to 5 year period of time! Quite a different view from that of the previous generation.

Specialized Skills

A world of rapid knowledge growth and hyper-innovation is leading to a big increase in the specialization of every skill and career. That makes for a vicious circle which further compounds the problem of the emerging skills crisis.

How are people impacted? Every profession, every career and every job is being sliced and diced into multiple subcategories. The days in which you could hire one professional or skill set and expect that individual (or individuals) to master all that needed to be done are over. No one can be expected to know everything required of them—and everyone is becoming a specialist.

As things become more specialized, the simple laws of supply and demand suggest it will become more difficult to access the specialized skills you might need to run your business. Instead, you will find you have to access ever more rarified and specialized talent, probably on a part-time, contractual basis.

Chapter 5

What's the Impact?

"Foresight is the secret ingredient of success,
because without foresight we cannot
prepare for the future."
Futurist Magazine

Clearly, things are going to be changing far faster than ever before.

I've long used two statistics that I think sum up the rapid rate of change that is occurring, and the impact on the world around us:

- A study out of Australia looked at issues surrounding innovation; the report concluded that 65 per cent of children in pre-school today will be employed in careers and jobs that don't yet exist. I find that to be a stunning number, and even if it is only partially true, it is a pretty significant barometer of the change yet to come.

- Futurist magazine observed that the pace of change is now so fast that most people will find themselves not only in four or five different jobs in their lifetime, but in four or five different careers. It's not just young people who are graduating into a world that is continually different; those of us already in the workforce will also see regular career changes.

Overall, we share one thing in common as a result of the trends outlined in the previous chapter: we will need to learn to deal with change in all aspects of our lives. To keep up with change, we will have to be able to constantly learn, relearn and learn again. As Lewis Perlman, a well-known educator, observed years ago, "learning is what most adults will do for a living in the 21st century."

One thing is certain: any degree of comfort you might have with respect to your current career, or the industry and marketplace in which you work is probably misplaced. What you will be responsible for tomorrow will be very different from what you do today. The very nature of your career, the organization you work for and the skill sets you will require are going to undergo some pretty fundamental changes. You need to realize that even if you don't adapt, the world around you will!

What impact will the trends discussed in the previous chapter have? Let's have a look.

HYPER-INNOVATION

An era of sapiential circles, massive knowledge growth, rapid scientific advance and "smarter" types of things have led to a world of relentless innovation or 'hyper-innovation.'

New products and services are being brought to the marketplace faster than ever before. The best way to excel in this new environment is to hop on board the hyper-innovation train, and ensure that your career, attitude, skills and capabilities are set to take advantage of the opportunities the future presents, rather than the threats and challenges it imposes.

Hyper-innovation is coming about not simply because of the faster sharing of new scientific discoveries; it is also being driven by the emergence of what we might call a "global innovation feedback loop." In every industry, profession and field of endeavor, news about the latest innovations and developments are shared on an almost instant basis, which has forever changed the idea of a product or service "life cycle."

> *By some estimates we will see as much change in the 21st Century as we saw in the last 20,000 years.*

Why is this so? In the past, many companies kept track of the evolution of the products and services sold in their industry and marketplace through very careful analysis of the activities of their competitors, through review of specialized industry publications and magazines or through their own competitive intelligence research efforts. If a competitor released something new, it was analyzed, reviewed, digested and dissected. It could then be improved upon, developed, enhanced and brought to market with the label "new and improved."

Yet the pace of innovation wasn't terribly fast in most industries; "time to market" moved slowly, a reality which worked to the advantage of those who were leaders at innovation. They could thunder into a market with a brand new product or service, knowing they had the luxury of time before their competitors could catch up. In that age, the idea of "sustainable competitive advantage" was a worthy business concept, one much sought after. The secret to success in the business world was to do something that your competitors would not be able to match for quite some time. In that way, you could capture and own a market for several years, leaving your competitors in the dust.

No longer.

Now, the evolution of innovation within a market can be tracked online, in real time. Innovation has gone naked—there are no longer any secrets in any marketplace. Companies merely need to tune into the global innovation feedback loop to understand how their industry is evolving, and what they must do next to go one step further.

Where is the global innovation feedback loop? It's all around you—in online discussion groups involving customers and consumers, in weblogs or blogs, on websites, in online industry newsletters and in the scientific community's discussion lists and forums. We've entered a world in which "people in the know" are talking about "what comes next" to such a degree, anyone who learns to tune into its signals can now understand leading-edge innovation, in real-time. (Clearly, though, a lot of people are not tuned into the loop, because they are just like the frogs on the road in Texas—they've stopped watching the future, and don't follow what it is telling them.)

Nowhere is the era of hyper-innovation and a global innovation feedback loop more apparent than with the consumer electronics industry. We've seen the emergence of sites such as Gizmodo and Endgadget, among many others. Gadget aficionados and industry players can track new product announcements and rumors on a daily basis. Leading edge cellular companies, camera manufacturers, television and home entertainment companies not only track what their competitors are up to, but "leak" information about their upcoming plans to these sites, hoping for some type of consumer awareness and marketing bump.

The result of this feedback loop is an industry in which those who care to watch the trend seem to know what everyone else is doing—and that type of feedback loop is rapidly coming to every industry, and will affect every organization. With that being the case, every participant in an industry must monitor the loop and struggle to keep up and stay ahead of the curve. Which leads to the need for relentless innovation, or hyper-innovation.

How big is the impact of the global innovation loop? The barometer is once again found with the consumer electronics industry, one of the first to be impacted. Minolta, a long-time manufacturer of camera equipment, has dramatically shortened the life cycle of their digital camera product line, simply because the pace of innovation affecting this type of product is now so rapid. They are now completely focused on the reality that they must be prepared to release entirely new, revolutionary, groundbreaking products every six months, instead of every year or two.

Imagine the mindset and the organizational culture required to maintain such a furious pace of development! That's the reality set to emerge in every industry and marketplace as hyper-innovation solidifies its hold on the world.

HYPER-COMPETITION

The reality of hyper-innovation is a product life cycle of a year or two at best, for most industries. In some industries, we're already witnessing product life cycles of six months or less, which will become common in many more markets. In turn, this hyper-innovation will lead to increased competition in every marketplace.

Yet a furious pace of competition doesn't come only from rapid innovation; it comes about from a variety of other factors as well. Organizations which might have faced one or two competitors in the past are now suddenly faced with dozens, if not hundreds, of competitors. These new challenges are due to the rapid increase in global knowledge exchange, rapid scientific advance and hyper-innovation.

A new organization can walk into a marketplace and become a competitor faster than ever before. Companies used to know who their competition was—there was often a friendly atmosphere at industry get-togethers, as long-time veterans shared their thoughts and ideas about the state of the world and their industry. Associations and conferences focused on a clearly defined and easily understood target audience. It was easy to keep on top of new developments, since the field of existing competitors was well-known and well-defined. Many individuals found themselves working for four or five different companies in their industry, moving from competitor to competitor as their career and skills changed.

This is no longer the case. Organizations are increasingly faced with regular and ongoing upheaval as new competitors walk into their market and attract their customers, and as rapid developments permit the emergence of new markets which never previously existed. To survive and thrive, and to keep on growing, organizations must be prepared to do the same thing these new competitors are doing. They must also be prepared to adapt and enter into new markets on a continuous basis.

The organization of tomorrow will find that it must constantly redesign its business, continually revisit its strategy and change and morph itself into new markets and new product lines almost overnight.

CHANGING CAREERS – FROM MASSIVE SPECIALIZATION TO COMPLEXITY COORDINATORS

This world of rapidity doesn't just affect companies, industries and markets; it is also having a deep impact on the future of every career, and the skills that will be expected of people within those careers.

In a world of ever-increasing complexity, it is impossible for anyone to cope with and master all of the required knowledge within a particular profession or skills area. The result is an increased degree of specialization within what were once broad areas of knowledge. Every profession from human resources to engineering, from agriculture to medicine will see more niche oriented positions.

As more and more professions become subdivided to deal with a world of massive specialization and complexity, we will see the emergence of a new type of skill and career: individuals who excel at understanding all of these specializations and who know how to access the right skill at the right time for the right project. We might call them "complexity coordinators."

Career Specialization

As the world becomes more complex, many people will find their areas of responsibility become more tightly-focused and aimed at more narrowly defined areas of specialization.

For example, while in the past we had "human resource professionals"—individuals expected to handle a wide variety of issues—the field of employee and career management has now become far too complex for any one individual to manage alone. Today we have career counseling specialists, as well as people who focus on training and development, others who are specialists in corporate use of instructional technologies and others who spend their time on labor or industrial relations issues, not to mention pension and group benefit managers, as well as career planning experts. One profession, many specialties.

So it is with accountants. In the past, professional accountants were expected to be able to master a core set of functions and capabilities. Yet today, we've got forensic accountants, tax accountants, information technology accountants, as well as many other specific niches of specialized expertise, including accountants who have become experts in all the intricacies of Sarbanes-Oxley! No single accountant can be expected to master all the professional knowledge required of them; it would be impossible to do so today.

> ### Some Specialty!
> *Thomas Hefti at the Swiss company Givaudan, is a flavor specialist scientist. He has a repertoire of 20,000 synthetic taste sensations—300 for strawberry alone. The company is responsible for one of every five global artificially flavored foods.*

Then there is the medical profession, which continues to fragment into hundreds, if not thousands, of sub-specialties. While at one time family doctors could be expected to deal with just about any issue put in front of them, today they are far more likely to send you to a specialist for anything but the most routine type of medical issue. The reason for this? They simply can't keep up with the rapid growth of knowledge in the world of medicine, and the ever-increasing number of new medical discoveries, techniques, treatments and drugs. Every medical professional is being impacted in the same way.

Now consider manufacturing. Mechanical engineers might once have been able to apply their skills to any number of potential situations. Today, they might focus all their professional skills and expertise on the implementation of new manufacturing methodologies, becoming a "process transformation specialist." Others might focus all their skills on newly emerging smart, hyper-connected remote maintenance technologies. Still others might excel at understanding how to take advantage of specialized expertise located in Asian countries, and knowing how to use this talent within a North American manufacturing company.

These are but a few examples. Every profession, every career and every job is being sliced and diced into multiple subcategories. We must be prepared to develop the skills and attitude to cope with such a trend, not to mention the ability to determine in which specialty to focus.

Complexity Coordinator

At the same time that we are witnessing ever-increasing career specialization, within many professions we are also finding a need for people to take on the role of what could only be described as a "super-project manager." This person needs to:

- understand what each specialist does;
- know which specialist to call on and when;
- make sure that all the specialists work together to the common objective; and
- be able to assess whether others need to be called in.

This role involves a whole new set of skills, and will involve such a degree of unique ability that I've come to call them "complexity coordinators."

While some individuals will find their chosen profession is undergoing a constant evolution into multiple specialties, others will learn they must master multiple specialties to survive and prosper. They must be able to take on a wider variety of roles and responsibilities, and will be expected to pick up an ever-increasing number of new skills. Their expertise, career, and indeed, their entire job will be to excel at managing the complexities of the world around them.

The best analogy for a complexity coordinator? A symphony conductor!

JUST-IN-TIME KNOWLEDGE

With the rate of change now enveloping us, people are expected to be able to master new topics and issues at the drop of a hat. They must be able to quickly assess and understand the new knowledge emerging in their profession, industry or area of specialty, and incorporate that knowledge into their skill set. Mastering the skill of learning the right thing at the right time is what I have come to call "just-in-time-knowledge." It's the ability to instantly and immediately access and develop needed knowledge in a hurry, a skill that will become an absolute necessity in a world of rapid change.

The best example of an industry and profession impacted by the need for just-in-time-knowledge occurred with the recent worldwide emergence of SARS. When Severe Acute Respiratory Syndrome first appeared on the scene, health care professionals discovered they needed to quickly learn about a wide variety of complex medical issues. Many medical associations found themselves scrambling to put together educational conferences that focused on the many different aspects of SARS, ranging from medical training and diagnosis and crisis management, to public safety and education issues. The exchange of online research information occurred at a frenetic pace; the number of research papers examining SARS soared. The global medical sapiential circles were abuzz with activity.

The impact of SARS on the sheer volume of medical knowledge was dramatic. Indeed, we have never seen the medical world evolve from having literally no information about a new disease, to a situation in which the collected global information available on SARS was estimated to quickly exceed the extent of global medical knowledge that existed in 1965.

Of course, every medical professional in SARS-impacted regions was expected to understand and master much of this new knowledge, very, very quickly. They had to learn all about SARS, just-in-time.

We can expect this type of demand for instant knowledge acquisition to become more frequent in the future, and we should prepare for it accordingly. A world of rapid knowledge advance implies that a greater number of people will be expected to learn instantly about new topics, issues, products or strategies.

A SHIFT FROM TACTICAL TO STRATEGIC SKILLS

With hyper-innovation, hyper-competition, changing careers and just-in-time-knowledge demands, organizations must very carefully assess the skills, role and value of their staff and executives. They have to operate smarter and better, and simply can't afford any of the inefficiency and wasted effort that still exists today.

At this point, we are on the cusp of another perfect storm—one that is resulting in the ongoing commoditization of human capital—and no one is immune. The commoditization has already been seen with the wave of offshore production and outsourcing that has overtaken the economy over the last decade. Yet so far, mostly clerical, routine jobs have been affected by these trends. The next big group to be affected: those whose jobs have long demanded certain professional skills and insight.

The *Chicago Tribune* recently stated the trend perfectly: "It is becoming clear that CPAs, management consultants, attorneys and health professionals who have traditionally been insulated from global market forces will be faced with competition as they have never seen before: bright, driven people capable of offering comparable-quality service at perhaps a tenth the cost of their developed world counterparts."

We live in a time when it really doesn't matter where certain types of work are performed. In Bangalore, India, you can find a one-square block area where a variety of skilled professionals are providing services ranging from home mortgage processing and approval, medical CT scanning and chip design and software development, right next to another group that is processing tax returns.

The *Chicago Tribune* went on to cement the reality of this new economy, noting that we "...are now witnessing the emergence of a global market in which an ever increasing portion of the developing world acquires the education and opportunity to provide skilled-labor, including professional services of almost every kind at a world class level."

Organizations are finding that everything is becoming far more challenging, resulting in a need to constantly refocus their workforce and reduce their cost base to stay competitive. Faster competition will continue to lead to a greater degree of structural, ongoing corporate change that will make today's corporate restructuring pale in comparison.

> **Critical Skills in an Era of Constant Change**
>
> *Bayer Corp and National Science Foundation Survey found that these were the most important skills sought after in new hires.*
>
> *The ability to:*
>
> - *solve unforeseen problems on the job*
>
> - *adapt to changes in the work environment*
>
> - *do their best work in teams*
>
> - *continue to expand skills as the company changes and/or grows.*
>
> *The Bayer Facts of Science Education VII: The State of American's New Workforce*

As competition increases, organizations will be forced to continually undertake bold new actions to retain market share. They will continue to relentlessly attack their cost structure, seeking to squeeze out new efficiencies and achieve cost savings. They will pursue new external partnerships with the aim of outsourcing as many ongoing functions and responsibilities as they can. And the only staff they will keep on hand are those who help them change, determine future directions, implement strategy and steer the organization into these uncharted waters—all of which involve a type of strategic role. All the rest will be tossed aside to third party organizations, itinerant or temporary staff, and other part-time fleeting relationships.

What this means to you is that the very idea of "job security," which has already come under attack in the last several decades, is but a quaint idea from a time that is long, long gone. As organizations continue to refocus their workforce structure for an economy that demands ever-increasing productivity, flexibility and innovation, they've come to realize there are many routine, day-to-day, transaction-oriented functions that need not be undertaken in-house. They've learned that with global connectivity, they can now access highly talented professionals wherever they might be. To survive and thrive in the future, you must ensure you make a transition in your career from a tactical role to one that is more strategic. Increasing reliance will be placed on those who can bring real results to the organization, and there will be fewer concerns about casting aside those who don't, because they'll be easily replaced from the global marketplace.

A DIFFERENT TYPE OF CO-WORKER AND EMPLOYER

What does this lead to? We are rapidly entering an era in which the very nature of the corporate organization is undergoing a subtle but significant shift. It will no longer be an entity with the full range of skills and staff that exist in most organizations today. Instead, it will consist of a small, core group of strategic staff who define the goals and activities of the organization and who orchestrate access to temporary skills on a continuous basis.

There is a simple reason for this: if you take all the trends we have looked at and put them together, things are becoming far too complex for any organization to do everything that needs to be done. Organizations are going to increasingly rely on short-term, specialized, expert talent, simply to accomplish what is necessary in a world of heightened complexity.

Nomadic Workers

According to the US Department of Labor by 2010 most engineers will not have a full time job. Instead they will be "itinerant project professionals" who work on a wide variety of short term assignments for various organizations.

Because of hyper-innovation, organizations will find it necessary to rapidly enter new markets, and might not have the specialized expertise to do so. Hyper-competition will lead to a sudden necessity to ward off a new competitive challenge, which can only be accomplished by bringing on some experts who will help them in a hurry. Rapid new scientific advances that impact the professional role of much of their staff might mean they need to do some pretty fast R&D to stay in the game—and there will only be a few people worldwide with the specialized knowledge and expertise who can help them out.

> ### Hollow Companies
>
> *Metro International, which puts out small, local newspapers in major metropolitan areas around the world, is typical of the type of organization we will see in the future. The Company is really just a brand— they make nothing and outsource everything. They employ few reporters, and simply buy their content on the open market. They don't own any printing presses; they simply outsource that to organizations in the markets in which they operate. They don't even own any distribution networks, instead preferring to use the services of those who already have well entrenched networks in the cities in which they operate. Noted the London Times, the Company "operates, in effect, as a network orchestrator."*

In a world of global connectivity—and in particular, in which young people are fully prepared to accept new, alternative working models—organizations will be able to access this needed talent on a moment's notice, wherever that talent might be. They will be supported by a global, temporary workforce that will help them for a short period of time and then move on, ending their temporary relationship with the organization.

In the future, your fellow co-workers will be something and someone very different; your relationship with them will be short-term, fleeting in nature and project-oriented. You'll find that there will be many different co-workers; they will come and go like visitors, as will you. You might not ever really "meet" any of them, other than in a virtual sense. And you will not have a job but rather multiple projects, short- and long-term that taken together will define your career.

As this changed organizational structure takes hold, your future success lies in understanding this model, and figuring how and where you best fit in.

IS THERE AN EMERGING COMPETITIVE DISCONNECT?

There is one thing in common with all of the issues above: we, and the organizations we lead/work for, need to accept rapid change, and need to respond with agility and flexibility to the coming opportunities and challenges.

Sadly, I think there are a lot of organizations and individuals who will fail to rise up to this challenge. History is littered with the remnants of those who have failed to adapt to change. Going into the future, there will be many more who will fail to anticipate what comes next, and who won't plan for incessant ongoing change.

The result will be an ever-increasing competitive gap between organizations in every industry. We will see the emergence of some organizations with the leadership smarts who know they must evolve and innovate at the rate the world and the future demand of them. And then there will be the rest; those who will continue to go forward into the future, driven by their aggressive indecision, motivated by their unwillingness to change, and guided by their blindness to the trends and challenges that will impact them.

The latter will gradually find their markets become smaller, and their opportunities less significant, as their nimble, future oriented competitors pass them by. They will find their lack of a forward-looking culture results in them being overtaken by those with massive change agility.

We can expect pretty significant shakeouts in every industry as the future unfolds, because some will adapt to these emerging realities, and many others will not. Your key goal is to ensure that you—and the organization you lead—escape such a fate.

C h a p t e r 6

Leading the Future

*When it comes to the future, leaders must create a
compelling sense of urgency.*

The future is your foe if you fear it.

That's perhaps one of the best sentiments you could adopt to lead
yourself, and your organization, into the future. The phrase implies
a mindset in which you turn threat into opportunity, and in which
you turn challenge into potential.

The trends outlined earlier make it clear that we are in an era that
requires leaders with the skills to prepare their organizations for a
future that is rushing at us faster than ever before. That's why
enhancing your leadership skills with the ability to focus on the
future is becoming critical, and why the ability for future-planning
is becoming a critical career capability.

Leaders help people make sense of what is happening around them, shake them out of their complacency and give them a clear path for the future. They establish a sense of momentum to carry the organization forward. They get their people thinking about the future and acting on their observations.

They do this by establishing an overall corporate culture that is forward-thinking, innovative, open-minded and focused on future success.

MANAGEMENT OR LEADERSHIP?

To respond to the reality of the world of change, you need to ensure that you and your organization are forward-looking and forward-thinking. It is critical to get into a leadership frame of mind even if most of what you do involves day-to-day management responsibilities.

> ### The Opposite of Management Is??
> *"What's the opposite of innovation? Management. Management is about making things come out the same. Projects require management. Innovation requires leadership. You can't manage people, creativity or ideas. You can give them leadership, however."*
> Dean Kamen, Inventor of the Segway

Some people use the terms management and leadership interchangeably, yet they involve distinctly different traits and responsibilities when it comes to the future, change and innovation. Managers are involved in the day-to-day direction of an organization. They ensure procedures are followed, required actions are taken and everything runs as smoothly as possible. Management is a critical skill, one not easily attained, and when it is done well, can cause an organization to shine. A great manager is akin to being the first mate of the ship, steering the organization on a daily basis through difficult, choppy and often unpredictable waters.

Leadership is entirely different. Leaders provide an overall sense of direction for the organization. They inspire individuals to pursue opportunity. They change the frame of mind and frame of reference for the organization's goals. From this perspective, a leader is the captain of the ship defining where the boat should go, before the voyage actually begins. They are future oriented, innovative and adaptable.

In essence, leaders define the future by establishing clearly defined goals; managers implement the future by translating those goals into specific day-to-day action steps. Many leaders are also managers; however many managers lack leadership skills. You'll enhance your opportunity, and that of your organization, if you can become a leader as well as a manager.

> *A Critical Leadership Skill For Our Time?*
> *Having the ability to make decision through ambiguity.*

ARE YOU A FORWARD-ORIENTED LEADER?

It has been said there are three types of people in the world: those who make things happen, those who watch things happen and those who say, "What happened?"

Let's take a look at each of these, keeping in mind the question: when it comes to leadership, which one am I?

Future-Blindness

I've encountered many organizations through the years that have sat back after some sort of dramatic, earth-shaking change and asked, "What happened?" In other cases they have been affected by slow and gradual change, yet have failed to adapt to the new circumstances which surround them.

All of them seem to share what I call the Three Monkeys' Approach to Leadership: it is best if staff sees no evil, hears no evil and speaks no evil. It's best if they are kept in the dark, focusing on today and not worrying about tomorrow. These organizations have developed a keen sense of future-blindness; and they are the ones that sit back in shock, after the fact, when rapid innovation and change has decimated their marketplace and industry.

Nowhere has this future-blindness capability been more tuned to perfection over the last several years than within the music industry. It remains a fascinating case study in which an entire industry adopted the Three Monkeys' approach to the future. All the signs indicated rapid market and innovation turmoil: customers were revolting against the business model, sales were plummeting and the media was scathing in its condemnation of music industry executives for refusing to recognize their industry was in dire trouble and in need of significant change.

Yet music industry executives preferred to remain blind to the trends enveloping their industry. No one seemed prepared to talk about the reality that the global innovation feedback loop meant there would soon be a flood of small little devices allowing people to carry around thousands of songs. No one dared listen to the customer to learn that an entire generation was rejecting the idea of buying music on shiny little round discs called CD's. No one dared confront the reality that the very value of a music album had declined precipitously in the mind of the customer as online music swapping took off.

The entire attitude of the industry was one of "we dare not speak the truth"—and look what happened to them.

Future-Avoidance

I've also encountered many organizations quite busy watching what is happening all around them, but who are not quite prepared to cope and adapt to the change that is occurring. They seem to have developed some type of "change-immunity": they know there is some pretty big stuff happening to them, but they aren't quite ready to confront the reality.

I remember dealing with an entertainment company (not in the music industry, incidentally). Their market was in upheaval; there were significant customer challenges, and there was a tremendous degree of turmoil within the organization. Ideas had become stale, innovation was dead and change was unacceptable. Their once-lofty reputation was suffering as a result of their inaction evidenced by the constant criticism from opinion makers.

To their credit, the leadership saw the signs of change, and gradually came to recognize they needed to do something. A cultural shift was required; a focus on the reality of the future was necessary. Senior management contacted me, and after some discussion I was invited to talk to their staff about how they might embrace the change that was causing so much havoc, and how they might spin this change into opportunity.

As I do in many situations, I met with these executives in advance so I could frame the issues, understand the challenges and determine where the opportunities might lie. But when I did that, a funny thing happened: they made it clear to me, in no uncertain terms, that I shouldn't cause any undue alarm within the organization. Yes, the future was rushing at them and they agreed things were pretty challenging, but they didn't think it was a good time to wake up their staff to what was really going on. They didn't want to cause any undue concern; they thought it was just too difficult and too painful.

The result? I spent my time with them, but never had the opportunity to get into the real issues. We skimmed the surface; we barely confronted reality.

If you look at this organization today, the problems have only become worse. They still see no evil, while the evil rushes all around them.

Future-Embracement

I contrast these two situations with the approach taken by the executive director of a major professional association who approached me to give the keynote address at their annual conference. He was fully aware that if his members did not take some pretty significant steps in terms of their role within the organization, they might be faced with a degree of career extinction—not just career upheaval and change, but actual extinction.

This industry was rapidly witnessing the impact of the global outsourcing revolution. At the time, it was readily apparent that if the professional members of the association didn't increase their value to the organization by making a transition from a tactical to a strategic role, they would likely find a huge number of their jobs quickly moving offshore. Already, significant components of their industry were gone.

His strategy? I should come in and scare the hell out of them, which I did extremely effectively. I outlined the global trends impacting their industry, and how certain components were due for certain extinction; how the perception of the role they played and the value they brought to the organization meant they were most often viewed as a simple commodity, a service that could be easily and effectively "offshored" at a lower cost.

Yet the executive director also advised that I shouldn't focus solely on the threat and challenge in front of members of the association—it was critical they understand the clear and present opportunities in front of them. The executive director made it clear to me that I would hit a home run with him, and with the crowd, if I effectively outlined to the audience what they should do to respond to those realities. In effect, the approach should be to "scare the hell out of them, and then let them know what they should be doing to confront and manage the future to their benefit." (Incidentally, I hit the ball out of the park, and since that time I have used this approach as the cornerstone for many of my future-oriented talks.)

Leaders of Today

I believe leaders today need to adopt this same philosophy. Heaven knows we've seen too many organizations lose sight of where they are headed, with a basic inability to respond to new competition and rapid innovation.

Weighed down with excess costs, bureaucratic processes and inefficiencies and an aversion to risk, they end up seeing customer defections and a resultant loss of market share. This leads to a renewed focus on panic cutting—cost cutting merely to survive—

and haphazard attempts to do something new to grow the top revenue line. But by that point, it is usually too late.

Leaders of today need to embrace the future in order to avoid such knee jerk reactions. They need to prepare their organizations for the future by defining direction, encouraging innovation and effecting change. They need to establish an overall organizational culture in which everyone is firmly focused on the future while managing the present. In this way, threat is turned into opportunity and agility becomes a cornerstone for success.

Through the years I've seen many such leaders, and have observed that they have several common characteristics. They possess:

- the ability to link the corporate mission of today to the major trends and developments that will influence the organization through the coming years;

- a leadership style that encourages a culture of agility and allows for a rapid response to sudden change in products, markets, competitive challenges and other business, technological and workplace trends;

- the ability to establish and encourage an organization-wide "trends radar" in which all staff keep a keen eye on the developments that will affect the organization in the future;

- the skill to create a culture of collaboration in which everyone is prepared to share their insight, observations and recommendations with respect to future trends, threats and opportunities;

- the ability to form a corporate culture in which staff are encouraged to not only deal with the unique and ongoing challenges of today, but are open and responsive to the new challenges yet to come;

- a performance-oriented focus in which people are encouraged to turn future challenges into opportunities, rather than viewing change as a threat to be feared.

In a survey, the Association of Graduate Recruiters in the UK identified these skills as the top skills for the future. In my opinion the list clearly identifies the key attributes for all forward-thinking leaders. In addition, it clearly outlines the attitude, skills and capabilities that leaders should engender within their staff.

- *Self-awareness*
- *Self-promotion*
- *Research skills for ideas and opportunities*
- *Decisiveness and action planning skills*
- *Adaptability and flexibility*
- *Negotiation skills*
- *Networking skills*
- *Teamworking skills*
- *Written communication skills*
- *Oral communication skills*
- *Presentation skills*

WHAT DOES A FORWARD-THINKING LEADER DO?

Listing these attributes of a forward-thinking leader is one thing, but how do you go about deciding if you are where you should be in becoming a forward-thinking leader?

One of the first things you must do is to assess the readiness of you and your organization to deal with the challenges of the future. To help you do this there are a number of careful, probing questions you must ask of yourself and of your organization:

- **Shifting you and your organization's culture from one of threat to one of opportunity** – do you have an attitude toward the future that is focused more on defining opportunity than avoiding threat?

- **Defining a vision and desired outcomes** – have you established a great vision of where you want to be in the future, given the rapid rate of change?

- **Communicating and embracing the vision** – have you shared the future with the people in your organization? Do they know where they are going and how they are going to get there? More importantly, do they buy into the future, and embrace it with the same sense of passion that you carry?

- **Promote innovation, flexibility and adaptability** – are you open to new ideas and ways of doing things? Do you feel you have an open and forward-thinking corporate culture?

- **Develop communication feedback loops** – do you listen to and encourage others to listen to each other in terms of the trends they see? Do you have a means to collect, review, and communicate the ideas generated?

- **Making decisions makes a difference** – do you encourage staff to make decisions? Have you "empowered" your people?

- **Reward innovation-based success** – does everyone have a stake in achieving these opportunities, and are they rewarded for future thinking?

These questions form the foundation of an innovative, forward-thinking leader. The key is to translate the results into specific directions and actions. Here are some things you should be thinking about.

Shifting You and Your Organization's Culture From One of Threat to One of Opportunity

When I began speaking to organizations about the future many years ago, I spent much of my first year focusing on the very real threats emerging for the folks in the audience. I'd concentrate my remarks on the market and competitive threats coming about in their industry. I'd focus on the new business models set to cause havoc. I'd talk about the looming trend to "offshoring" and outsourcing as organizations continually examined the value of their staff. And I'd close with a rousing call that they need to figure out how to respond to these threats in order to survive.

In retrospect, I scared the hell out of a lot of people during that first year, but didn't offer much in the way of advice as to what they should do. I came to realize this after a fellow came up to speak with me after one particularly scary keynote. "I certainly agree that we're faced with a lot of threat," he stated, "but shouldn't we be trying to focus on how to turn those threats into opportunities?"

Ba-bing! A light went off in my head that day, and it has forever changed the way I approach—and explain—the future. Certainly, the world of the future is full of threats that could derail our business, cause havoc with our plans, and result in instability in our careers—but only if we choose to let this happen. We can't simply focus on the threats; we have to learn to turn the existing challenges into opportunity.

That's why, as a leader, you should carefully ask yourself: Are you in the right frame of mind when it comes to the future? Or are you like a "deer-in-the-headlights," in terror of what the future holds? If so, shift your focus so that you are constantly probing the trends unfolding around you, with a view to determining how you can capitalize on them.

Defining a Vision and Desired Outcomes

The next most important thing a leader can do is define a sense of direction, establish goals and set objectives for the organization. Without a clearly defined future, an organization will find itself wallowing in indecision; most efforts will focus on solving the mundane and trivial issues of today, rather than pursuing the grand and significant opportunities of tomorrow.

What is truly amazing to me is that there are so many individuals, and so many organizations, caught flat-footed by the future simply because the leadership hasn't established where they are going. To help get this point across, I often tell a story provided to me by one of my sons.

> **Leaders as "Futurists"**
>
> *The Institute for the Study of Accelerating Change at Stanford University identified the attributes of a "futurist." The list provides excellent guidance as to the skills, attitude and insight of a forward-thinking leader.*
>
> *1. One who habitually develops future goals and plans (near-, intermediate- and longer-term);* **future-oriented**
>
> *2. One whose present thoughts and behavior are strongly influenced by future expectations (with regard both to things they can change, and things they probably can't, such as major trends and their possible discontinuities);* **foresighted, response-able**
>
> *3. One who contemplates a range of possible world models and future scenarios and seeks to find and advance preferable ones, while avoiding undesirable ones (e.g., "ask not what the future can do for you; ask what you can do for the future.");* **proactive, normative**
>
> *4. One who forecasts both predictably regular and predictably chaotic change using scientific methodology (logic, analysis, and empiricism) in scientific, technological, global, national, cultural, and personal complex systems;* **forecast-oriented, falsifiable methodology**

My two sons are very aware that their dad has a different type of job which often includes "going out and talking to large groups of people." (That's how my one son put it into perspective.) At one time, my youngest son, then in grade 3, came home from school with a short story they had just read in class. "I thought you might be able to use this in one of your speeches," he told me, handing over the brief story of Alice and the Cheshire Cat. And what a story it is!

> *Alice came to a fork in the road.*
> *"Which road do I take?" she asked.*
> *"Where do you want to go?" responded the Cheshire cat.*
> *"I don't know," Alice answered.*
> *"Then," said the cat, "it doesn't matter."*
> *Alice in Wonderland, Lewis Carroll*

If an organization doesn't know where it wants to go, then it really doesn't matter what it is doing today! And yet that seems to be the reality with many organizations—they are at a fork in the road and don't quite know what direction to take, simply because they don't know where they want to go. They lack an effective leader who has them firmly focused on the future.

You need to clearly define the direction and vision of your organization, and the results expected once you get there.

Communicating and Embracing the Vision

Of course, a vision and outcomes are useless unless they are shared with everyone in the organization. Effective leaders do not shy away from telling staff where the organization is going, the plans they have for the future and how they think they need to get there— whether it is good or bad news.

Yet simply communicating the vision isn't all there is to it. You need to work hard to establish an overall degree of buy-in from everyone in the organization, so that your staff shares your passion for the opportunities that exist.

> *Forward-thinking leaders make time for their staff to work on the business, rather than simply in the business*

By sharing your vision and by getting them onside, you are giving your staff the opportunity to change with the organization, learn new skills and be proactive in their future, rather than reactive.

Promote Innovation, Flexibility and Adaptability

A forward-thinking leader realizes that in order to survive and thrive, he/she and their organization must be in a frame of mind that can constantly respond to rapid change.

They promote and support an open-mindedness throughout the organization that encourages regular and constant examination of business processes, markets, products and customer service methods. They encourage a line of thinking that suggests there is always room for improvement in the way the organization works and get things done. They've ensured the organization has evolved to such an extent that its day-to-day business processes can instantly adapt to new requirements and demands.

How does such an organization come about? A forward-thinking leader sets out to demolish the use of the phrase, "We've always done it that way," replacing it with the mindset, "Why not try something different?" They implicitly encourage a culture of agility; one in which people aren't tied to the procedures and methodologies of the past, but are prepared to adjust what they do and how they do it to cope with the rapidly emerging realities of tomorrow. They provide a sense of direction that leads to a widespread recognition that in order for the organization to be prepared to cope with hyper-innovation and hyper-competition, it had better be prepared to change the way it works, thinks and acts—and do it regularly and rapidly.

There are many organizations that don't have this capability. They spend their time in countless meetings, focusing on the mundane and routine matters of today. Decisions take a long time, if they come at all. Managers rule the roost, with the result that success comes to those who don't rock the boat and who don't provide any original thinking.

> *Leaders turn "clear and present dangers"*
> *into "clear and present opportunities."*

Does the later describe you and/or your organization? Or do you encourage fresh thinking? Are you able to quickly change a point of view? Do you recognize this as a good capability?

Develop Communication Feedback Loops

Many individuals are not prepared to take on a forward-thinking role; their skills are tactical, role-oriented, and are aimed at achieving certain day-to-day tasks. And yet, their insight can be critical to future success.

The world of business is far too complex for any one individual to clearly assess all the trends that might influence the organization. A successful forward-looking organization has a culture in which everyone feels responsible for watching for the signs, trends, directions and innovations that will spell future opportunity and threat. A leader needs to provide what is necessary to promote and encourage both the culture and skills that support such thinking.

A purchasing manager, responsible for ensuring that procurement budgets are met and that the best purchasing decisions are made, might hear a comment from a supplier suggesting a certain trend down the road. A salesperson might witness a new competitive challenge in the marketplace that senior management is not aware of. Other staff might see some small signs that could seem inconsequential and trivial, yet in the larger picture could have a significant effect on the organization. All of these individuals should be able to share their insight and observations with the rest of the organization. Staff should be encouraged to discuss how they think this will impact the organization, and what should be done to implement/change/use these observations to reach the end goal.

Do you encourage your people to discuss future trends with you? With others in the organization? Do you discuss your future observations with others? Do you have a time and/or place set aside to discuss/review/share observations that you and your staff have? Promoting this type of communication in your organization ensures that everyone is part of the group and that they understand they can make a difference.

This is such an important issue that we will revisit it later on, when we take a look at the idea of a 'trends and innovation loop.'

Making Decisions Makes a Difference

Observations about trends are great, but if you don't act upon them they are useless. Does your staff have the ability to make decisions that make a difference? You can't become an innovative, forward-thinking and flexible organization if people don't think that they can make a difference, and if they don't actually have the capacity to effect change, even in a small way.

There has been a lot of talk over the last several years about the need to "empower people," yet the sad fact remains that quite a few staff within organizations have little authority to do anything new. The organizational culture holds them back; they've never been encouraged to get really involved in effecting change. If they do attempt to do something different, they quickly discover that the organizational sclerosis that exists within the organization clogs up any ability to move forward.

> ***Email on the GO***
>
> *GO Transit, a commuter rail service in Toronto, Ontario recently implemented a system that notifies regular travelers via e-mail when a train is late. The idea came about after a frontline staff member informally implemented such a process for various customers as a courtesy.*

Are you a leader that can push decision-making to the lowest capable level? Do you understand that providing your organization with the direction and culture needed to cope with a more complex future is going to take the efforts of everyone? Break down the clogged organizational arteries that exist in your organization, and instill a sense that things must change to deal with the future.

Reward Innovation-Based Success

Today, the reward systems of many organizations are not based on the future success of the organization. Instead, people are rewarded on how well they achieve their day-to-day tasks.

Managers are rewarded for their short-term efforts in achieving short-term objectives. Overall, executive performance is based on matching the expectations of stock market analysts in achieving short-term quarterly results. Staff are evaluated on whether they've balanced the books and whether current sales production targets have been met.

All of these are perfectly valid methods of evaluating performance; yet, if they are the only measures of success, then something is clearly lacking.

As a forward-thinking leader you need to ensure your people are motivated and rewarded for their efforts to adapt to the future, and for their ability to effect change. This needs to be enshrined in both the formal and informal methodologies that are in place.

TELL THE TRUTH

There's another very important leadership attribute when it comes to the future: the ability to tell the truth about what will happen if the organization and/or its people don't change.

Leaders today can't be afraid to tell it like it is; the challenges are too real, the threats too immense and the opportunities too diverse and significant. Yet I continue to encounter far too many leaders— whether middle management or senior executives, entrepreneurs or government bureaucrats—who clearly aren't prepared to lead their organization through turbulent times. They simply don't feel comfortable creating a compelling sense of urgency for change based upon the reality surrounding them and the future coming toward them.

A REAL, FORWARD-ORIENTED LEADER

Forward-oriented leadership is a rare and precious capability; it takes time and effort to develop this unique skill. And as with all things, one of the best ways to further understand the skill is by looking around you, and thinking about those you have encountered who have mastered the capability.

In my own case, I was quite lucky, in that I worked for a leader who I now recognize as being one who was a forward-oriented leader long before the rate of change of today had encompassed our world. Twenty years ago, I was invited to join a unique project team in the major organization in which I worked. Our goal was to define the parameters for the future—how would our company be impacted by the rapid, relentless change that would occur through global connectivity?

The fascinating thing is that this fellow had identified the emergence of the Internet as a pretty "big thing" some twelve years before the rest of the corporate world caught on. Talk about insight!

As the team came together, he presented us with some very unique challenges to address. How would the skills and knowledge required of us as professionals be affected? How would our marketplace change? What opportunities might exist that could be capitalized upon, and what unique threats would emerge? How might we as an organization change the way we worked, and the way we were structured, to accommodate a world in which information would be shared at a blinding speed previously unseen?

Thinking back, I now clearly see all the elements of great leadership. And I saw more. He didn't know exactly what was happening, but knew it was big, and that something had to be done. He didn't have the expertise to deal with it on his own, so he established a team and a culture that could help him to do what needed to be done. He wasn't ashamed to admit his ignorance of the issues at hand, but carefully listened and observed.

And once he understood what was happening and the implications, he established a crystal clear and great vision.

At that point, he rallied us as troops in a common cause, and encouraged us to take risks in order to achieve our goals. He created an environment that supported our seemingly wild and crazy ideas, and provided the support that permitted our activities and decisions to have an impact. He rewarded us for our efforts, and praised us for our passion.

He was a forward-oriented leader, and I learned a tremendous amount from working with him. Sit back for a moment, and think about whether you've encountered such individuals through your career, and use them as an inspirational torch for your own future-oriented leadership.

Creating an Innovation Culture

Innovation is creativity implemented!

Great leaders instill great passion for the future.

Clearly that was the lesson learned from the greatest leader that I ever worked for. I've long thought about what this fellow taught me, and over time I came to realize that in addition to being a great leader, he also had one other extremely important trait—he established a culture that supported regular and ongoing innovation by everyone on the team.

In doing so, he helped to propel the organization into the future by creating an environment that encouraged everyone to take responsibility for getting it there.

I once sat back and thought about how he did this, and the more I thought about it, the more I realized that there was a method to his madness. There were certain things that he encouraged us to do, and attitudes that he encouraged us to adopt. He fostered in us an intense curiosity as to what was going on around us, and made us really think about what might come next. He chose the team carefully, seeking us out because we had already earned a reputation as rebels. He immediately encouraged us to collaborate and share our ideas on a continuous basis.

He framed our potential in stark terms—making it plain to us that a willingness to change was critical to the future success of the firm, but that we were up against some pretty significant barriers in trying to cause that change to come about. To succeed, we'd have to have the courage to break the mold—and by realizing that, we became tremendously excited about our mission.

Talk about a perfect recipe for an innovative environment! What he had really done was crystallize in my mind the essence of innovation as six key cultural attitudes.

THE SIX-C'S OF INNOVATION STRATEGY!

Clearly, innovative organizations exist because they have an organizational culture that is based on an innovation mindset. As a leader of your organization, you are responsible for creating and nurturing this culture.

> *Are You Innovative Enough?*
> *If you are like most companies, probably not. A survey of major organizations by Accenture found that while most CEO's indicated that innovation and creativity were at the top of their agenda, only 6% felt that they were successful at actually achieving it.*

You can do so by pursuing the Six-C's of innovation strategy: provide for curiosity, creativity, collaboration, change, courage—and by creating excitement every day!

Curiosity

Intense curiosity is critical to innovative organizations—their people spend a huge amount of time thinking about the world around them and making observations about where they might be headed in the future. They are motivated to discuss the results of their curiosity, and how their findings might provide opportunities for their organization.

> ### The Essence of Curiosity
>
> *I recently read a novel called Operation Roswell—a bit of science fiction that explored what would have happened if "aliens" really did crash-land in Roswell, New Mexico over fifty years ago. One character in the book made what I thought was a brilliant comment summarizing the way I think about the world: "I've learned that you never know what might be important down the road, so I ask questions and file away the answers."*
>
> *I spend a huge amount of my time asking questions and thinking about what I see occurring everywhere around me. I try and interpret that information in order to discover or assess an important trend.*

Innovative organizations fuel this culture of curiosity and encourage their people to look for trends, signs of change and opportunities everywhere, whether from observations within the local neighborhood, things seen during day-to-day business activities or from a brief news story observed online. It might come from the insight provided during a conversation with a customer, or from the research done when preparing for a staff presentation. Whatever the case may be, there is a degree of fresh thinking and resultant curiosity that become the seeds for an innovative opportunity.

You should encourage curiosity throughout your organization. Everyone, including you, should have an understanding that they should be constantly watching the world around them. What you are looking for is insight and observations that might lead to ideas. As a well know Noble Prize winner, Dr. Linus Pauling observed "the best way to have a good idea is to have lots of ideas."

Creativity and Rebellion

Curiosity leads to creativity. Yet curiosity must be nurtured to create innovative ideas, and creativity will only flourish in an organization if the right mindset exists.

That's a problem for a lot of organizations, because they tend to view innovation as an event, rather than a state of mind. They announce a big innovation drive, encourage a lot of ideas and then fail to act upon them. They do this regularly with the only result being the breeding of a lot of cynicism throughout the organization.

An innovative organization is full of people who continuously look at the world around them and think, "Why are we doing things this way—could we not do it better if we tried something different?" Having asked that question, they then focus on imaginative ways to tackle the problem. They use creativity as their method for achieving innovation, and use metaphorical crayons as a fuel for that mindset. Truly innovative organizations promote constant creativity; not only that, they fuel the fire of that creativity by encouraging rebellion.

> ### *Demand Your Crayons Back!*
> *To get into an innovative, creative frame of mind, you should demand the right to use crayons again! Most of us were very creative as young children. We were given crayons at an early age, and were encouraged to be as creative as possible. Yet as soon as we hit grade one or two, someone took our crayons away. With that, much of our opportunity for thinking creatively disappeared. In order to become innovative, you've got to make sure you get your crayons back!*

In some cases, it may be difficult to spark creativity in an organization. That is when leaders seek out the 'rebels.' Rebels are leading-edge trendsetters who are often at odds with the typical corporate direction or commonly accepted practices. They're the radicals in the crowd, eager to cast off the past because they already live and participate in a future that is very, very different. They're busy tearing apart the conventional business models that have guided organizations for ages; they have different ideas of the nature of the product or service that is sold, and they are all too eager to change everything around them to create the future as they see fit.

Many of these lone wolves have an attitude, outlook and approach to life and business that is completely at odds with those around them. However, innovative leaders realize they can learn from them and are willing to listen to what they have to say, because these rebels are often the heart of many a great innovation.

Here is one such example. A food manufacturer was trying to find out how to improve the changeover time of one of their assembly lines, when they hit upon a novel solution: bring in an Indy race pit crew to show them how. Their thinking was, who has better mastered the talent of "quick thinking, quick work" than a group of people who can instantly change several tires in a highly-coordinated team effort lasting only a few seconds? It was an offbeat solution, but it certainly did the trick.

As a leader in your organization, you need to encourage your people to be creative, and you should keep an open mind to what might sometimes seem quirky or unusual solutions to difficult problems—they may lead to innovative opportunities. Encouraging creativity is encouraging innovation.

Collaboration

Another important trait that innovative organizations possess is that of collaboration. Leaders listen to the rebels, have them share their ideas with the others in the group, listen to what others have to say and encourage dialogue on an ongoing basis, not only among the rebels, but among everyone on the team.

Innovative thinking thrives on the sharing of ideas and the regular exchange of insight. All of us learn from experience, and we all learn from each other. It is through the process of sharing information on trends, opportunities and ideas that groundbreaking innovations occur.

Through collaboration, you can also demolish the skepticism that may exist in your organization. Phrases such as, "That's the dumbest thing I ever heard," "That's not my problem," "You can't fix that" and "It won't work" sometimes override the new ideas being proposed. You won't succeed at all if you have a corporate culture that stops innovation dead in its tracks.

You need to take the time to engender and build an informal, "open-door" culture that promotes regular and ongoing contact among all staff. Feedback, complaints and observations, as well as a culture that provides for the sharing of leading-edge trends, challenges and opportunities, needs to be encouraged. Individuals who excel at working well with others and who see open communication as the fuel for innovative thinking will help lead your organization into the future.

Change and Opportunity Masters

Innovation also comes from those who realize that a true, real, sustainable result comes from doing things differently. These individuals don't look at the emerging challenges of the future as a threat to be feared, but as an opportunity to be pursued! They are open and adaptable to change, and have abandoned all pretense of "change-blindness."

> ### Participation is Critical!
> *According to Director Magazine, 75% of all organizational change programs fail, because employees feel left out of the process and lack motivation to participate.*

These people come from the premise that the worst phrase to ever be used in the world of business is "We've always done it that way." This demonstrates their passionate belief that the worst thing an organization can do is cling to the past, and they work aggressively to destroy any such attitude. Tony Blair, upon winning the leadership of the UK Labour Party in 1994, clearly demonstrated his passion for going forward, proclaiming: "I want us to be a young country again. Not resting on past glories. Not fighting old battles." He couldn't have framed the opportunity for new, fresh thinking in a better way.

Leading organizations and their leaders encourage their people to relentlessly probe what they do and what the organization does, continually asking how they could do things better. They focus on the future and the opportunity it brings, rather than thinking the current way of doing things is "good enough." They encourage the desire to constantly change that which needs to be changed and to take advantage of new opportunities.

You should immediately stomp on any type of change anti-virus that exists within your organization. There should be a clear and undeniable message that everyone must be prepared to change to respond to the demands of the future rather than concentrating on the past. As the CEO of Home Depot observed: "The landscape is strewn with retailers who had a great business model and got locked into the past versus building off the past."

> ***Don't Look Back***
> *"A company must become entirely free of denial, nostalgia, and arrogance. It must be deeply conscious of what's changing and perpetually willing to consider how those changes are likely to affect its current success."*
> Harvard Business Review

Courage to Take Risks—and Make Decisions

Without risk, there can be no innovation. Innovative organizations, recognizing this reality, work to instill a sense of courage among their staff, and encourage them to take risks.

Is your organization in that frame of mind? Possibly not—through the last several years, many organizations have allowed their "risk budget" to become seriously depleted. In doing so, they've replaced their innovation oxygen with the smog of aggressive indecision. Beset by war, terror, a challenged economy and much uncertainty, they have permitted the emergence of a culture that doesn't encourage innovation heroes. Worse yet, their culture has become so degenerative, they can't even make any decisions.

I certainly see this as a consultant and as a speaker. While I used to be regularly booked as far as a year in advance, now some organizations are booking me just a few weeks before their conference or event. In other cases, I've had proposals go out to clients for strategic planning sessions, only to be befuddled by their inability to come to any closure on the matter.

> **The Importance of Courage**
> *"Courage is an essential value for creativity and innovation...without courage, open and challenging discussion would not be possible."*
> Aventis Pharma Australia, Statement of Values

Why? Because uncertainty has led to a degree of decision stagnation.

Pummel this trend to the ground before it goes any further! Make sure your organization runs by timelines, deadlines and clear goals and objectives, and that people learn to re-embrace the risk that comes from making a decision. Carefully ensure your culture provides for regular decision-making, not deferral and never-ending discussions.

You are probably wrestling with a few issues that have been around for far too long. What should you do? Encouraging risk-taking is one method to end complacency, as is rewarding failure. Remember: there can be good decisions and bad decisions, but making no decision will get you nowhere.

Create Excitement, Every Day!

Last but not least, innovative organizations are excited about the future!

No doubt there have been many challenges over the last few years, with recession, war, terrorism and other problems. As a result, many people in the business community have lost their sense of purpose and their passion for the future. Innovative organizations have continued to move beyond this; they've established a common cause to achieve a common goal to attain. They engender a sense of excitement in their staff, and establish a sense of purpose in every day-to-day activity. They show their people that innovation should happen all the time and everyone should be involved in it.

THE IMPORTANCE OF A FORWARD-THINKING CULTURE

When I think back to the best leader that I ever worked for, not only did I realize that he had set us on the perfect road to innovation, he had also helped us to become more forward-thinking in our views. He shifted our focus so that we were continuously thinking about what might come next, and what we might do about it.

That would be an important thing for you to consider within your own organization. Do you have an organizational culture that encourages your staff to keep one eye on the future while they focus on the necessary work of today? Do you encourage staff to better themselves so that their skills will meet the needs of the organization as you move forward? Do you have a good sense of the type of people you will need in the organization to move it forward?

An organization firmly focused on the future doesn't get there by simply having a leader who is aware of where things are going and who establishes a sense of direction. They get there by backing up the leader with a staff that is as equally supportive of the drive toward the future.

> ### Chinese Proverb
> *If you are planning for one year, grow rice.*
> *If you are planning for 20 years grow trees.*
> *If you are planning for centuries, grow men.*

That can be a big problem to solve, since far too many organizations today are extremely focused on the present, and concentrate solely on the achievement of day-to-day tasks. They are wallowing in indecision, and suffer from too much complacency with respect to the future. They're just like the frogs in Texas! In this type of organization, those who best manage the company are those who rise to the top of the heap.

Worse yet, these organizations have let their staff drift into a culture of complacency. They've allowed an attitude of "We've always done it that way" to creep into place, and that phrase has become the foundation on which they strategize and prepare for the future.

Yet adaptive, successful organizations think differently. They consist of a majority of staff in which one eye is focused on the future at the same time as they work on the realities of today. There is an understanding that the organization faces great challenges, but also significant opportunities. Everyone understands that they need to be watching for and capitalizing on the wide range of opportunities emerging around them at the same time that they focus on their current responsibilities. In this way a corporate culture emerges that is both future-oriented and present day focused

Innovative, forward-thinking organizations have great leaders who help to get the organization out of a state of ennui, and who truly become oriented toward "what comes next." As a leader you need to establish and promote this type of culture.

The Trends & Innovation Loop

The key to innovation is simple—anticipate the future and act upon it.

Great leadership and an innovative culture—is that all you need to go forward? Not really. You must also have an ongoing awareness of the many trends and issues which will affect you. Your analysis of these trends is also crucial to your ability to spot opportunities, for it is through this process that you can identify new areas for innovative thinking.

Earlier in the book I outlined what I believe to be the eight major trends that will shape our world through the next many years. Yet in addition to these major trends, there are many other trends that might affect you. Some are industry specific, while others will impact broad portions of society. Some might be insignificant to the vast majority of people and to organizations, but could have very serious repercussions for others.

To succeed with the future, you must carefully watch for the trends that will impact you, and determine how to react. But how do you go about actually keeping track of all these trends? How do you ensure that your organization examines these trends and turns them into useful ideas and suggestions?

The trends and innovation loop, described in this chapter, may help to get you started. I've developed the loop over the years, after carefully analyzing how highly adaptive and innovative organizations watch, react to, and act upon the trends they observe. The key lesson to learn is that in such organizations, everyone bears responsibility for this process, because a forward-thinking culture has become the backbone of these types of organizations.

WHO IS RESPONSIBLE FOR WATCHING THE TRENDS?

In many organizations, planning for the future is done by a group of people dedicated to the task. These "strategic planners" spend their days trying to understand trends and work to put strategic directions in place for how to respond to these trends. Yet all too often they work in a vacuum—they don't have the vast range of information the rest of the organization possesses. Without that information, these planners don't really know what might come next.

For example, they might not be aware of innovative new sales methods involving the competition, because the sales force has never been asked to provide such insight. They may not be aware of new customer service methodologies put in place by the competition, simply because no one has ever been assigned responsibility for watching this stuff. They might miss the signs of forthcoming industry-wide competition because purchasing managers, aware of new products becoming available in the supply chain, don't bother telling anyone else in the organization.

A forward-thinking and innovative organization sets out to change this perspective and methodology. They make sure everyone throughout the organization understands that even though their responsibilities might involve countless number of day-to-day responsibilities, they must also play a role in the innovation loop.

THE INNOVATION LOOP

Clearly, organizations and the people within them need to learn how to become more forward-thinking.

They need to become attuned to the challenges and opportunities of the future, rather than mired in the mundane issues of today and the problems of the past. The trends and innovation loop outlined in this chapter can provide you with a methodology and a cultural way of thinking to help you implement the observations and ideas discussed so far in this book.

The loop provides every member of the organization with a way to monitor and share information on leading edge trends, and turn their collaborative, forward-oriented insight into realistic strategies, plans and action steps.

To make the loop work, there must be clear understanding that everyone in the organization is responsible for:

- observing important trends that might impact the organization;

- sharing what they see;

- thinking about these observations in terms of the potential they might bring to the organization;

- generating innovative ideas; and

- helping to put those ideas into practice.

Without this type of organization-wide understanding, most efforts at innovation and dealing with the future will be doomed to fail.

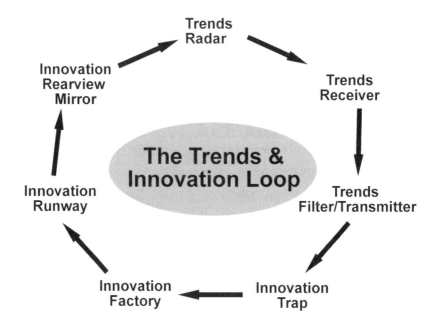

Let's take a look at the elements of the loop.

Trends Radar

Innovation comes from the ability to see the obvious, so the first step in the loop is to establish a form of "trends radar" that keeps you attuned to the future.

Everyone throughout the organization should be prepared to constantly look for new developments and opportunities that might impact your business or market, and that might provide opportunity for innovation. They should also be watching for trends, issues or signs that might indicate a potential threat or looming challenge. Everyone needs to understand that having good radar can help the organization spot future opportunities and act upon them, as well as do what is necessary to ward off and deal with potential threats.

What should your people be looking for? Anything that could potentially impact the organization, such as a sign that a competitor is launching a new customer support initiative, or perhaps an announcement about a new industry supply chain effort that might signal an opportunity for partnership. It could come from something as innocuous as a comment from a customer to a salesperson on something they've seen in terms of sales of a certain product.

In addition, it could involve observations from a speaker at a conference on industry trends that mean nothing when taken out of context, but when combined with other information, signal a rather seismic industry shift. It might involve information indicating a sudden, rapid change in customer expectations, or a change in the geographical reach of a competitor's sales force. It could be a news story, or an item published in an industry journal, or anywhere else.

> ### Growing Markets
>
> *I carefully watch a huge variety of trends, and have learned to tie together different observations into an overall, broader trend. Here's a good example:*
>
> *I know from my observations of demographic change that Hispanics will soon make up 18% of the population in the United States, up from 13% today.*
>
> *Knowing that, I was intrigued when I came across a recent survey that indicated that while many are comfortable speaking English for most day-to-day activities, they are not as comfortable speaking English when it comes to financial services.*
>
> *Tie into that another observation that many Hispanics operate outside the traditional financial system—only 65% have bank accounts! They also remit some $30 billion per month to relatives back in their home countries, outside of the traditional financial networks. That spells opportunity, and that is why at their recent annual meeting, the Bank of America stated that 80% of their growth is going to come from ethnic markets/marketing.*
>
> *Linking together all of these trends provides me the ability to provide my financial clients with unique, in depth insight into how their markets will change in the future.*

An effective trends radar can also be formalized to a degree, wherein specific signals are tracked for signs of significant change. This might include, for example, monitoring specific new scientific advances or technical developments that might transform the industry. It could also involve keeping on top of specific developments in other industries or professions that might impact the organization. It may even include watching what the world's leading experts in the industry are doing, and analyzing what they are talking about.

The key point is that the organization has made a decision to track the future. The message is set such that everyone understands that trends need to be watched, both to spot opportunities for innovation, and to determine actions to respond to emerging challenges.

Trends Receiver

Having your people watch for trends, developments and issues all around them is the first step in the loop. The second is to instill in them the confidence to share these observations with everyone in the organization. This second step in the methodology has two components: a cultural willingness to share information and a mechanism to collect the information.

Firstly, a forward-thinking organization establishes a culture that supports the continuing and regular exchange of knowledge pertaining to new developments. The leadership provides a clear and unequivocal message that not only is everyone responsible for spotting trends, they must also play a role in providing their insight into these trends so the potential impact on the organization can be properly assessed. The task of encouraging the communication of ideas can sometimes be quite challenging, but it is a critical step in moving your organization forward.

Secondly, as everyone becomes involved in watching and analyzing new developments in the world around them, they must be able to share this information with key players throughout the organization. Without a good receiver for what your radar has identified, you won't succeed in discovering new areas of opportunity, and might not be able to identify potential threats.

There are many different tools and methods by which the information can be gathered and shared. You could use the corporate email system, knowledge databases or the internal intranet. In addition, regular strategy and staff meetings, annual and semi-annual conferences or other regularly scheduled get-togethers are good methods to gather and share information.

Think about it this way: to assess the impact and opportunities of future trends, you want to establish your own internal "sapiential circles" or "knowledge-sharing groups."

> ***Collaborative Innovation***
>
> *A good example of operational innovation based on information collaboration? The Wm. Wrigley Company launched an internal sales knowledge resource center that provides for archiving of previous discussions/queries related to sales strategies, markets, opportunities and leads. The company estimates it has saved its sales agents about 15,000 hours in research time.*

It is important to remember to develop a receiver that fits with your organization's working style; the receiver is as much a culture as it is a tool. If you make it too complicated and formalized, or too simplistic and lackadaisical, it may discourage people from participating.

Trends Filter/Transmitter

A good trends receiver is critical to gathering all of your people's observations, but without a good filtering and transmission system, the ideas will go nowhere.

What is the trends filter/transmitter? It is the process of taking the observations and ideas generated from the receiver, sifting through them and finding the ones that might be important. Again, there must be a cultural willingness to digest the vast number of observations from the outside world, remembering many could be irrelevant, and only a few might truly indicate something worthwhile. But it isn't only the filtering of the observations and ideas; it also involves the process of sharing the best of those ideas in order that something might actually be done with them.

What could this process look like? It could be a formalized methodology where the organization's leadership encourages staff to share their observations on a regular basis at lunch sessions or at regular strategy or staff meetings. There could then be a specific "innovation group" that analyzes and filters the information. Another process could include implementing an internal Weblog application or other collaboration system where your people share their thoughts on the impact that each observation might have on the organization.

> ### Inexpensive Knowledge Tool
> *An important point—organizations now have the capability to capture, transmit, share and collaborate on ideas in ways that have never previously been possible. Inexpensive Weblog software, for example, can provide the foundation for an organization-wide collaborative knowledge tool, for minimal cost.*

The key to making the filter/transmitter work is ensuring important observations and successful ideas make their way to senior executives. Studies have shown that many of the most innovative ideas come from middle management, yet fail to be implemented because of senior management inertia. The corporate culture and methodology should provide support for the sharing of the best ideas amongst all staff or particular groups of staff, so that there can be further debate, analysis, research and creativity applied to those ideas. In this way, the filter/transmitter provides for a weeding out process, with the potential for further ongoing examination of the best ideas that the radar and receiver have provided.

> ### Chocolates are for Sharing
> *Great ideas are like boxes of chocolates—
> they are always better when you share!*
> *Found on the Monroe County,*
> *Florida School Board's Website*

Innovation Trap

Many of the ideas your trends radar might spot and share won't make sense, and might be meaningless in the grand context of things. But on occasion, critical information will emerge that might spell a brilliant opportunity or a significant threat. When that happens, you must be able to turn those observations into actionable plans.

> **Knowledge Strategist**
>
> *Chuck Ferguson carries the title "knowledge strategist" at Sun Microsystems, and is responsible for fostering a culture of information exchange within the organization. One of his key innovation tools was the establishment of an "innovation repository" on the company's internal network. Employees are encouraged to regularly contribute the random ideas that they might have had on issues of customer service, market opportunities or cost reduction.*

You should think of the innovation trap as the organization's process of taking the best potential observations from the trends filter/transmitter. At its heart, this is a creative process.

The innovation trap process could include involving multiple "innovation team leaders" who bear specific responsibility for creative analysis. In this process, regular meetings could be held in which the objective is to look at identified trends, figure out what they might mean and determine what should be done about them.

This process involves asking a lot of questions, such as:

- Why is this trend occurring?

- What might it mean?

- What is behind it?

- Does it infer something else, and if so, what?

Encourage people to be creative, to generate ideas, to think outside of the box. Establish a culture in which brainstorming is encouraged, both formally and informally. Regardless of the methodology, the goal is to identify the trends that will have the greatest impact on the organization.

Innovation Factory

The next step is to move these trends along to the innovation factory, where concrete, actionable plans can be put together to implement the ideas.

Your innovation trap can come up with a lot of great ideas, but if you are like many organizations, you'll fail to see them turn into something real and sustainable. Most experts agree that new innovative ideas fail in many organizations, not because of a lack of imagination, but due to a basic inability to turn ideas into actionable items. Corporate inertia takes over with new ideas; innate resistance to change causes fundamental problems with the ability of people to comprehend and accept those ideas.

The innovation factory is a cultural willingness to embrace change. It is also the methodology by which new ideas are translated into real business activities and initiatives. The factory is the process by which the ideas are examined in further depth, in order to understand how they will be launched, what types of barriers might be encountered along the way, and the best methods by which they might be successfully introduced. In essence, the factory could be considered the process of 'pre-implementation brainstorming.'

An innovation factory likely already exists within your organization for the process of new product or service development and delivery. Many organizations have long excelled at this part of the innovation methodology, since they have had a structure in place that helps them take new products or services to market. Most likely, this involves a specialized research and development group.

But where organizations really need to focus their energies— beyond product/service R&D—is in learning how to turn their best non-product/service ideas into action plans. If the ideas involve new ways of working, opportunities for business process transformation, or new methods of solidifying current customer relationships, then the organization has to work harder to build the innovation into something real.

Innovation Runway

Once the ideas have been translated into concrete, actionable plans, you'll need a method to ensure they are properly launched and integrated into the organization—the innovation runway. Actionable plans might involve experts at implementation and project management, and other individuals who can effect change within the organization.

> ### Setting the Tone
>
> *Years ago, a new managing director at the BBC set out to shake up the massive bureaucracy that existed within the organization. The motto he adopted to wake the organization up to the need for change? "Cut the crap, make it happen." It certainly managed to get the message through in a rather blunt and undiplomatic fashion, yet it did have the desired effect. He crystallized his change initiative into six easily identifiable key goals: maximize creativity, remain in contact with changing audiences, value people more, lead more and manage less, take risks, just do it!*

Innovation won't succeed if people think the status quo is good enough. If they see their resistance to change is rewarded, they'll continue fighting back. They have an almost Pavlovian response to change; if they can use the phrase, "We've always done it that way," and that phrase manages to stop change in its tracks, they'll continue using it.

The organization's leadership needs to set the unequivocal message that change is going to be constant, that change needs to be accepted and that everyone is expected to be at the forefront of implementing and driving change. Without this type of leadership, all innovation is set to fail.

This is where issues of change management and leadership come into play. Study after study has shown that most people are averse to any type of change; yet innovative organizations are those where change is welcomed and embraced. We'll re-examine the issue of implementing change in an upcoming chapter, since it is so critical to the process of becoming forward-oriented.

Innovation Rearview Mirror

To complete the process, place yourself in a position of continuous re-examination of your innovation success. You must constantly re-evaluate what you've learned, what you've implemented and how well it has worked. Use this process to enhance your understanding of how to be innovative by changing your approach for the next round of the innovation loop.

Innovation is everywhere—the problem is learning from it. That is why it is so critical to look back—you should be constantly accessing what you did right, and what you did wrong.

A LAST WORD

Trends-tracking and analysis can be a very powerful capability to possess. I spend a huge amount of my own time analyzing leading edge trends, whether it is related a specific client project, or part of my overall role of keeping on top of critical global trends.

However with the volume of information that exists today, it can seem overwhelming.

To manage the flood of information I receive, I've implemented a sophisticated software tool that has allowed me to build an internal knowledge database of the issues and trends I track. Vast amounts of information from various online newsclipping services and other sources flow into topic folders that I have set up - innovation, corporate culture, emerging trends, ethic issues, etc. I browse through the information on a continuous basis, and analyze what I see.

With this tool, I can quickly refresh my observations on a specific trend. I can go back at any point in time and review the information to pull together what's needed for my presentations, articles or material for media interviews. I can add my own commentary to specific articles and in an instant can pull up summaries of all the key points.

I have seen many of the most successful and innovative organizations with similar capabilities at their core. What has really made such systems successful is that everyone is involved. The trends tracking and analysis activity is an ongoing, regular process that has become a part of the very fabric of the organization.

People often admit to me after one of my future trends presentations that they find it difficult to keep up with the massive amount of information that is available today. Taking advantage of the various tools that are available makes dealing with this challenge much easier. It also allows everyone in the organization to participate in the innovation loop, which is critical to the development of an overall, successful innovative culture.

Changing to a Certainty Culture— Dealing with Aggressive Indecision

Success goes to those who get to the future first.

By this point, you understand that you need to begin watching and preparing for the future given that some pretty significant changes are set to come. You've given some thought to how you might lead your organization to ensure it masters the future. Finally, you have discovered the types of opportunities that can come from innovation.

You might be eager to get going—indeed, you may already have quite a few ideas on how to get started. Yet I still find that many organizations have yet to resolve one of their main big problems—the aggressive indecision that I defined earlier. Decisions are not made because of the uncertainty that exists.

To move your organization forward your people need to get away from their fear of making decisions, and into a mode in which they are prepared to go forward in the absence of certainty.

DEALING WITH UNCERTAINTY

How do you do this? First look at your organization and determine if it is "stuck." Here are some warning signs to think about:

- a business mindset averse to any type of risk;

- an absence of any new initiatives;

- an organization stuck in a rut, wheels spinning, and no one has even decided to call a tow truck.

Second, realize that aggressive indecision means you'll likely have to respond to external pressures faster than ever before. That's because while people are learning they can hold off making decisions until the very last minute, they are also learning they can still get things right by following this procedure. This process leads to a business cycle involving extended periods of frustrated waiting, followed by a blur of activity as organizations rush about to respond to the customers' demands for instant action.

Third, be prepared to change your corporate culture and work processes. You can't get mad at your clients for waiting for 2½ years and then making a decision, demanding you be there tomorrow. Make sure this process doesn't lead to an expectation gap—namely, your customer lives with aggressive indecision, and you still perform and deliver at the slow and steady pace that might have been appropriate in the past.

> **Lean Manufacturing**
> *There are certainly a lot of signs that many organizations are aware the future is unfolding around them, but are simply deciding not to participate. "Lean manufacturing" is a trend sweeping the industry, and is designed to bring more efficiency to results. Most major companies have aggressively implemented the concept, yet small and medium-sized manufacturers seem to be turning their back on the trend. A survey by the Society of Manufacturing Engineers indicated that though members could identify the benefits lean manufacturing would bring them, only one in four were pursuing it.*

Finally, make some decisions. Remember what it used to be like when you had the courage to do something? Let's call it the decision adrenaline rush. It's good—and it can be addictive.

Want to test it? Find the one big decision you've been deferring the longest, and decide one way or the other. Right now. Didn't that feel good? Try it again—immediately. See? Isn't that an amazing feeling?

You might not have made the right decision, and something could go wrong—but at least you've decided to start moving forward, rather than spinning your wheels in the mud. Battle aggressive indecision and you'll find you gain control over the future.

CHANGING TO A CERTAINTY CULTURE

There is hope if your company is in the indecision funk. There are several things you should do.

- **Recognize the problem.** Aggressive indecision can be an addictive vice, and like any other thing that isn't good for you, the first step is recognizing the problem.

- **Accept that uncertainty will continue to rule our economy.** The ability to make decisions in a vacuum has become one of the most needed corporate skills. Sure, things could go wrong as soon as you do, but that's the way the world works today. The important thing is you are again working to define the future, before the focus on an uncertain future does you in.

- **Accept the inevitability of change.** Back in the nineties, people believed we would see a lot of change in the business world. But now, with all that has gone wrong, it has become far too easy for people to convince themselves they won't be challenged by new business models, competitors or innovation. That's a dangerous attitude to carry around, and one that can also help doom you to a state of inertia.

- **Watch trends and react appropriately.** Now is not the time to let your radar down. Fact is, while you might be suffering from active inaction, your competitors might not. As a result, you are almost guaranteeing yourself some sort of surprise in the future.

- **Redefine goals, establish priorities and set targets.** Companies mired in the mud of aggressive indecision are often directionless and drifting. They've lost sight of the need to constantly innovate and establish new directions. As a result, most staff do not feel any compelling sense of urgency for change. Fix that in a hurry.

- **Re-examine your business strategy.** For the past several years, organizations have primarily focused on cost cutting, and yet taking the knife to operations can only go so far. Restate where you plan to go in the next several years, and communicate that vision and direction to your staff.

There are also a number of things you can do if your clients or colleagues are suffering from aggressive indecision.

- **Share the risk.** If uncertainty is killing many a business deal, see what you can do to minimize the fear.

- **Be clear about the potential downside.** If they aren't making a decision, then why not be more open about potential problems? If there are risks in the deal, be up-front about them.

- **Clearly define the benefits.** In an economy in which accountants rule the future, with every expenditure under the microscope, you've got to clearly outline the benefits and return on investment.

- **Scare them into action.** If they are stalling, put into perspective how their peers, competition or others in a similar position are moving ahead. People hate to be left behind, and if you can provide information about how others are charging ahead, it might spur some momentum.

- **Be prepared to move on.** Sadly, some people have become so bogged down with aggressive indecision, it might be time to cut your losses. If an existing client seems unlikely to do anything, you may do better spending your time opening doors to new clients.

- **Don't give up.** Continued aggressive indecision within your client or customer base can drive you to distraction. A continuously negative message can discourage you. In times like these, you must constantly battle the negative energy that aggressive indecision can cause you.

Bottom line? The natural human inclination when faced with something uncomfortable is to turn away from it—lingering uncertainty is the root cause of our aggressive indecision.

But we can't afford to do this any longer. Our careers, our companies and our future depend upon our ability to cope with a world of constant change. We'd better get used to it and take the time to learn the skills—and the attitude—which will help us thrive in this era of uncertainty.

An Action Plan for Change

Perhaps the only person who really
likes change is a wet baby

Leaders turn challenge into opportunity, and ideas into actions.

Clearly, it's time for some action! The status quo won't take you forward. To adapt to today's new realities, you will need to cause some pretty significant changes within your organization. That will involve getting people to alter the way they act, the way they think and the way they work.

Implementing change is one of the most difficult undertakings for any individual or organization: to me it seems many people have a built in "change anti-virus." The ingrained behavior they exhibit is not much different from the frogs I observed in Texas: they aren't quite able to change their focus in time to deal with the challenges they are presented with.

You need to start transforming your organizational culture to one that is forward-oriented and open to innovative thinking. You will also need to respond to trends that will present you with threat and opportunity. Responding to those trends will also involve ongoing change.

IMPLEMENTING CHANGE

Change of any sort, whether small or large, can be quite challenging to implement. Yet I've seen many leaders who have dealt quite successfully with the challenges that have been thrown at them because they have focused on changing the mindset of their people. Here are two notable examples:

- A major transportation company I was dealing with knew that they had to cause some fundamental changes in the way they operated to avoid the price commoditization ravaging their industry. All too often, they were competing on price, which increased their revenues but decreased their margin. The more they worked the more money they tended to lose. The leaders of the company realized that everyone in the company needed to understand what was happening to their marketplace and their company. They needed to get everyone to think about what changes could be made to improve their corporate situation. Standing out from their competitors could only happen if the mindset of everyone in the organization changed to one of innovation, and if everyone was willing to take the risk of trying something new.

- A major global food manufacturer was faced with significant price competition as a result of China entering the marketplace. They knew that they had to begin thinking about moving some of their manufacturing processes to China as many of their competitors had already done. They also knew that this would cause a great deal of concern, worry and stress throughout the organization since it had been manufacturing in North America for over 100 years. Again, the leaders of the company realized that if they were to continue to be successful things needed to change. They worked with their staff to help them understand what was happening in the global marketplace, and what impact that was having on the company. They set out to change the mindset of the organization to one that discussed and acted upon the challenges they were facing, rather than shying away from them.

In both cases, the leadership set the stage for change through communication and education. They knew that they would be up against instant suspicion, distrust and worry, and that to effect the change they had to be honest and forthright as to the need for dramatic action.

> ### The Changes We Have Seen!!
>
> *Pretend you have gone back in time to 1953. How would you explain some of these changes to your parent/grandparent?*
>
> - *Your daughter's tattoos and pierced eyebrow.*
> - *9/11 and the War on Terrorism; be sure to up date them on the Cold War and how it ended.*
> - *Explain Bill Gates, the browser wars, the dot-com bubble, Y2K bug.*
> - *Your wireless phone; and the games you can play on it.*
>
> *There are many more changes to come, but realize there are many that we have already survived.*
>
> *From www.speculist.com*

Given the ever-increasing rate of change around us, we have to constantly remind ourselves of the essence of a successful change strategy. Bringing change to bear involves understanding the challenges and barriers that will hinder your progress, as well as the methods by which you can smooth any ruffled feathers. It involves making sure everyone in the organization understands the change, the reason for the change and the effect of change.

Consider these elements when developing a strategy for change. You might find the process of change management far more straightforward.

Communicate!

Communicate, communicate, communicate—and then communicate some more.

Time and again, change initiatives have failed as a result of a simple lack of communication. All too often, those trying to effect the change have simply rammed the change through, without effectively explaining the reasons underlying the need for change, the implication of the change and the benefits that will come from the change.

Poor communication leads to all the classic signs of an ineffectual change process, ranging from suspicion, fear and confusion, to distrust and rumor. You will do much better if you spend as much time creating a "change communication plan" as you do structuring the details of the change itself. This plan will help ensure your message doesn't go off the rails.

Educate!

Communication is a key element to a successful change strategy, but education is just as important. You need to educate staff on what change means to the organization. Education implies information—and you can't have too much information.

Every person in your organization will have a different interpretation with respect to any type of change. It is important that you have detailed, comprehensive information available that clearly identifies the changes, how the changes will be implemented, why it is necessary to make these changes and any other pertinent information.

Try to deal with as many issues and areas of concern as you can. Hold information sessions or small group sessions where people can voice their concerns and questions. You must be prepared to answer all of their questions, regardless of how small or petty they might seem.

Anticipate Objections

As you send out your communications and present your education information, you will need to anticipate objections, misinterpretations and negativity. Recognize that no matter how hard you try, there will always be someone who expects everything will stay the same.

Many people seem to be driven by a rather simple outlook on life: whenever confronted with something new, they quickly respond we can't change things because "We've always done it that way." If you get right down to it, this statement masks the reality that they don't like change, don't want to have to deal with change and certainly won't accept change! They were born with a change antivirus that immediately rejects any invasion of their comfort zone by any type of new initiative.

 Given this reality, it is best if your change strategy takes into account the fact that you will have strong objections to your plans, regardless of how small or large the nature of the change might be. Take the time to understand the potential objections, and then document and communicate how those concerns are likely ill-founded.

Misinterpretation

Plan for the fact that people will misinterpret what you say.

Many change initiatives will run up the ingrained distrust that exists within the culture of many organizations. It's not surprising that many people will distrust you. After all, there is no doubt that people have been battered by an extremely negative corporate environment over the last few years, particularly as corporate cost cutting has come to be the key change initiative of many organizations.

In such an environment, any type of change you propose might simply be viewed as a part of that cost cutting agenda. You can counter this by being clear and concise. You also need to be firmly plugged into the rumor mill, and must be prepared to act immediately on any misinformation you might hear is being spread about.

Negativity

Hopefully you are trying to effect some positive change, and you can clearly outline a number of benefits that will come once the change is in place.

Even so, there is always a downside to any type of change, and you shouldn't hesitate to outline that downside. Make sure all your communications address any negative issues without hesitation. Don't try to sugarcoat them—people will see through that, which will only help to fuel the negativity that can come about from a poorly-managed change process.

Involvement!

Successful organizational change initiatives always involve the participation of those who are eager to see the change come about, or who have a stake in the successful implementation of the change. You'd do well to get these individuals involved as early as possible, since they will be very powerful allies.

At the same time that you involve those who want to see change, you will find you also need the support of those who are only marginally against the change. You'll make things easier for yourself if you spend a bit of time trying to turn them into supporters.

They might simply need some extra care and concern with the issues outlined above, since it might only be a lack of information that has them sitting on the fence. Spend the time to segment your audience and address their concerns appropriately, and you might find you are expanding your support base significantly.

Be Honest, Forthright and Ethical

Lastly, ensure your change initiative is based on simple human decency and values.

You set the tone and climate for change. If you are not seen to be a full participant in the change, don't share in any pain that it might cause or are seen to be aloof and isolated from the change, you'll destroy support quicker than you can say "off the rails."

You've got to be a full participant in the change, and ensure that fact is seen and noticed.

Chapter 11

Smart Frogs Go Forward

In order to get what you've never had,
do what you've never done

I never thought I'd be spending so much time thinking about frogs at this stage in my life.

Yet since the day I encountered those little critters in Texas—and watched their demise on the road—I've wondered about what advice that I might have given them to help them avoid their fate.

No doubt my basic message to them would have been simple: "Hey guys, enjoy the pond, but remember that things around this parking lot can change in a hurry!" In other words, focus on the present, but always keep one eye carefully turned towards the future.

Yet I would also have gone beyond that simple advice. Being the future-oriented sort that I am, I would have taken the time to chat with them about the type of future-oriented skills they should develop that would help them avoid their fate. Then I would have suggested they use these skills on a regular basis to develop the good sense of direction that has become so important in these days of indecision.

SKILLS FOR THE FUTURE

All of us possess important career and professional skills of some sort, and we know that these skills and the knowledge we possess will constantly change as the world rapidly unfolds around us.

Yet many other skills are becoming as important as these professional skills, if not more so. In many of my presentations, I provide guidance about the unique "soft skills" you need to develop to be able to cope and thrive in a world of constant change. Let's look at what I think are the most important "soft skills" you need to develop.

Know Your Skills, Strengths, and Capabilities

To go forward into the future, you must have confidence in who you are and what you can do. You must have a clear understanding of your skills, core strengths, and capabilities. This might not be easily done; circumstances around you might be changing so quickly that you aren't quite sure exactly what it is you can do!

I've certainly been in that situation. Back in the 1980's, when I was making the transition from being a full-time accountant with a major accounting firm to the unique future-oriented person that I am today, I had my own "skills crisis." I remember wondering:

- What skills do I have?

- Who might actually be interested in what I can do?

- What possible value might my unique way of thinking provide to organizations?

In retrospect, I realize I was going through the same kind of continual questioning and skills-probing that many individuals encounter today. In a world of constant change, one of the most difficult things to accomplish is being able to put your core skills, strengths, and capabilities into perspective, and to develop an understanding of how those skills can be applied to your career, your organization, and your future.

Think Opportunities, Not Challenges

You must develop a well-honed ability to research, identify, and seize opportunities. In effect, you need to grab the future and shape it, rather than being constantly shaped by the future.

To do this, you need to assess the future in terms of the opportunities it will bring to you and your organization, rather than concentrating on the challenges that it presents. That requires innovative thinking—you must constantly think of the opportunities surrounding you. Keep in mind there are countless ways to improve the way the business is run, how it performs, and how it functions. That is the essence of innovation, and it defines the opportunity for every individual. By thinking like this, you'll be in a state of constant opportunity identification, rather than in a state of distress and concern about what comes next.

Take the Initiative, Take the Lead

In this world of indecision and constantly changing circumstances, you must be able to take the initiative and take the lead. Yes, circumstances change and things are much more complex. However, while it might be more difficult to get things done in our new business environment, it should not be an excuse for inaction.

From this point on, adopt the attitude that you accomplish things and achieve results: break through the indecisiveness surrounding you. A key component of this skill is developing the ability to monitor, analyze, and adapt to future trends, and turn what you learn into concrete action steps. That way, you avoid becoming someone who steps back and asks, "What happened?"

Be a Collaborator

There is a need for instant knowledge in our world of constant change; that's why developing the ability of "just-in-time knowledge" is so important. Yet as you master this skill, you must also learn how to share what you learn by enhancing your ability to collaborate and work with others.

Are you in that state of mind? Perhaps not: I still find there are far too many organizations that have not yet achieved the "magic of collaboration." Staff and management continue to work in well-defined "silos" or departments, each responsible for their own piece of the puzzle and their own daily activities. There is little sharing of information and insight into the trends, issues, and challenges that might impact the organization along the way. There is no sense of overall spirit and no collective goal with respect to where the organization is going.

Yet as outlined in the trends and innovation loop, a collaborative culture is critical to becoming an innovative organization. To be an effective, forward-thinking leader, you must learn how to evolve your own skills, and that of your organization, to provide for true, effective collaboration and regular information sharing.

Make Decisions!

Future-oriented leaders apply their core skills and talents to constantly changing circumstances. They rapidly make decisions by identifying opportunities, despite a lack of certainty.

They have the courage to know that they might be right or they might be wrong—but at least they are going forward according to their best understanding of the circumstances. They are comfortable with risk, knowing that doing something in the absence of certainty is better than doing nothing in the presence of uncertainty.

Be Aware of Changing Relationships

Earlier in the book, I discussed one of the key trends that will define our future: the constantly changing and evolving relationships that surround us.

It is important that you develop the ability to sense how relationships are forming and reforming around you. What does it mean when the customers begin doing something different? What is the impact of a looming, large-scale industry initiative? What will happen as a new business model competitor comes into the marketplace and upsets the relationship apple cart that has long existed within the industry?

In my mind, this type of astuteness is another of the core attributes required to be a forward-oriented leader.

Develop Negotiation Skills

Negotiation implies the ability to create a "win-win" situation despite the challenges surrounding you.

How does this apply to future-thinking and innovation? From my perspective, future-oriented leaders assess these changing relationships, understand where opportunities might lie as they evolve, and determine how best to turn this relationship from a potential challenge into an opportunity.

How can you take the change occurring in your customer marketplace, and turn it into something that benefits your organization? How might you analyze the hyper-innovation occurring within your supplier base and partner with them so you can both succeed in an era of rapidly changing circumstances? How can you deal with the challenge of rapid knowledge growth and career specialization, and develop new external corporate partnerships that benefit both parties?

That's negotiation; not detailed, nitty-gritty contract negotiation, but rather the ability to take yourself and your organization through constantly churning, uncharted waters, and to come out on top.

Embrace Change

Another leading-edge trend identified earlier in this book, is "change de-resistance." Clearly, far more people will need to embrace change rather than shy away from it as they have in the past.

Which begs the question: are you able to cope with the change surrounding you? Are you able to change your goals, direction, and activities based on constantly changing circumstances? Not only that, but is your organization able to do this?

Enhance Development Ability

Of course, to be able to cope with and embrace change, you must be prepared to continually develop and enhance your skills.

You must be driven by an insatiable curiosity, a willingness to explore, and a desire to master anything new. That's your development ability—your understanding that to survive and thrive in a world of constant change, you must continually change yourself by enhancing who you are, and what you can do.

Be Self-Confident

Dealing with the future in a state of un-preparedness can be a shattering experience—or in the case of my frog friends, rather worse! That's why the trends radar outlined earlier is so important; by anticipating what comes next, you can do away with not being prepared.

As you tune your ability to track future trends that might impact you or your organization, you will develop greater confidence in your core strengths and capabilities. You will gain a greater appreciation of what you have and how you can apply it to the unique circumstances surrounding you.

The future is full of surprises only if you choose to permit that to be so. The alternative is to become a forward-thinking leader with confidence about the future—simply because you have a good idea of what is going to come next.

Promote Yourself

If going forward into the future requires self-confidence, it also requires that you be able to clearly project that confidence to others!

A forward-oriented leader sets the tone. To set the tone, you must make it known that you are prepared to take yourself, your organization, and those who work with and for you, into the future.

*   *   *   *

Over the last several years, I have found it fascinating how the "frogs in Texas" story has struck a chord with so many people. People often come up to me after my session, commenting on how I've just "nailed" their situation to a 'T.'

For example, a senior sales executive with a major global telecommunications firm told me that many of her customers were in a state of denial about the rate of change, turmoil, and opportunity coming to their industry. In another case, a senior executive with a major bank spoke with me about the changes occurring in the existing relationships in the financial services sector, and how he could get no attention for the need to change their momentum and their focus on how they dealt with the customer. Finally, a hospital executive decried the lack of understanding in the world of health care for the real challenges emerging in the future and the new solutions coming about by marrying looming hyper-connectivity with the opportunity for home health care.

The "frogs in Texas" story exemplifies people's reality: it makes evident that if we don't get off of this road of indecision and future denial, "there's gonna' be a big problem and it's going to be ugly." It helps us to realize that it is by becoming forward-oriented leaders, with the ability to spot the challenges and opportunities that are coming our way, that we can excel in an era of rapid change.

The "frogs in Texas" story is important, because it helps us understand how we can save our skin!

Could someone you know benefit by reading What I Learned From Frogs In Texas?

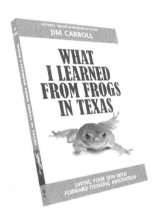

Purchase additional copies online:

www.FrogsInTexas.com

Customized Editions:

Do you need to spread around a little bit of innovation oxygen to your staff, customers or clients?

Jim Carroll can provide you a custom edition of this book that features your logo on the cover, and a customized four page "Foreword." Imagine having an introduction to the book written by your CEO, or a special introduction written by Jim that directly relates to your unique issues, concerns and opportunities. Contact Jim Carroll for further details.

905.855.2950   jcarroll@jimcarroll.com

FUTURIST, TRENDS & INNOVATION EXPERT

Keynotes, Workshops & Executive Briefings
Jim Carroll

Explore Your Opportunities,
Transform Your Culture,
Achieve Results!

Thought provoking, full of energy, up-to-the-minute and timely are just a few of the ways to describe Jim's presentations. He has the ability to energize people so they can discover opportunities for personal and corporate growth. He helps to stimulate creative thinking; provides thought leadership on cutting edge issues; encourages and motivates people to adapt to change; and provides detailed guidance and specific action plans that help to set the stage for innovative thinking.

Jim simplifies the future for people, and helps them to understand what comes next—and what to do about it!

Jim works with you and your people to determine your needs resulting in highly customized presentations.

Contact Jim today for a consultation to learn how he can help you!

905.855.2950   jcarroll@jimcarroll.com   www.jimcarroll.com